Date _____

Conditions

Weather

Terrain

Shelter

Shelter Constructed ☐

Type of Shelter

_____
_____
_____

Clothing/Coverings ☐
Waterproof ☐
Animal proof ☐
Sunproof ☐
Fire Started ☐

Map Sketch

Lat. _____ Long. _____

Food Inventory

Rations ☐
_____
_____
_____
_____

Water ☐
Hunting ☐
_____
_____
_____

Fishing ☐
_____
_____
_____

Foraging ☐
_____
_____
_____

Journey

Distance Covered

Trail Markers Used

Landmarks Sighted

Animal Prints

Party Member	Status	Injuries	Treatment

Date _____

Conditions

Weather

Terrain

Food Inventory

Rations ☐
_____
_____
_____
_____
_____

Water ☐
Hunting ☐
_____
_____

Fishing ☐
_____
_____

Foraging ☐
_____
_____

Journey

Distance Covered

Trail Markers Used

Landmarks Sighted

Animal Prints

Shelter

Shelter Constructed ☐
Type of Shelter
_____
_____
_____

Clothing/Coverings ☐
Waterproof ☐
Animal proof ☐
Sunproof ☐
Fire Started ☐

Map Sketch

Lat. _____   Long. _____

Party Member	Status	Injuries	Treatment

Date _____

Conditions

Weather

Terrain

Food Inventory

Rations ☐

_____
_____
_____
_____

Water ☐
Hunting ☐

_____
_____
_____

Fishing ☐

_____
_____

Foraging ☐

_____
_____
_____

Journey

Distance Covered

Trail Markers Used

Landmarks Sighted

Animal Prints

Shelter

Shelter Constructed ☐
Type of Shelter
_____
_____
_____

Clothing/Coverings ☐
Waterproof ☐
Animal proof ☐
Sunproof ☐
Fire Started ☐

Map Sketch

Lat. _____ Long. _____

Party Member	Status	Injuries	Treatment

Date _____

Conditions

Weather

Terrain

Shelter

Shelter Constructed ☐

Type of Shelter

_____

_____

Clothing/Coverings ☐
Waterproof ☐
Animal proof ☐
Sunproof ☐
Fire Started ☐

Food Inventory

Rations ☐
_____
_____
_____
_____
_____

Water ☐
Hunting ☐
_____
_____
_____
_____

Fishing ☐
_____
_____
_____

Foraging ☐
_____
_____
_____
_____

Journey

Distance Covered

Trail Markers Used

Landmarks Sighted

Animal Prints

Map Sketch

Lat. _____ Long. _____

Party Member	Status	Injuries	Treatment

Date _____

Conditions

Weather

Terrain

Shelter

Shelter Constructed ☐

Type of Shelter

_____
_____

Clothing/Coverings ☐
Waterproof ☐
Animal proof ☐
Sunproof ☐
Fire Started ☐

Food Inventory

Rations ☐
_____
_____
_____
_____

Water ☐
Hunting ☐
_____
_____
_____

Fishing ☐
_____
_____
_____

Foraging ☐
_____
_____
_____

Journey

Distance Covered

Trail Markers Used

Landmarks Sighted

Animal Prints

Map Sketch

Lat. _____   Long. _____

Party Member	Status	Injuries	Treatment

Date _____

Conditions

Weather

Terrain

Shelter

Shelter Constructed ☐

Type of Shelter

_____
_____
_____

Clothing/Coverings ☐
Waterproof ☐
Animal proof ☐
Sunproof ☐
Fire Started ☐

Food Inventory

Rations ☐
_____
_____
_____
_____

Water ☐
Hunting ☐
_____
_____
_____

Fishing ☐
_____
_____
_____

Foraging ☐
_____
_____
_____

Journey

Distance Covered

Trail Markers Used

Landmarks Sighted

Animal Prints

Map Sketch

Lat. _____ Long. _____

Party Member	Status	Injuries	Treatment

Date _____

Conditions

Weather

Terrain

Shelter

Shelter Constructed ☐

Type of Shelter

_____

_____

Clothing/Coverings ☐
Waterproof ☐
Animal proof ☐
Sunproof ☐
Fire Started ☐

Map Sketch

Lat. _____ Long. _____

Food Inventory

Rations ☐

_____
_____
_____
_____

Water ☐
Hunting ☐

_____
_____
_____

Fishing ☐

_____
_____
_____

Foraging ☐

_____
_____
_____

Journey

Distance Covered

Trail Markers Used

Landmarks Sighted

Animal Prints

Party Member	Status	Injuries	Treatment

Date _____

Conditions

Weather

Terrain

Shelter

Shelter Constructed ☐

Type of Shelter

_____

_____

Clothing/Coverings ☐

Waterproof ☐

Animal proof ☐

Sunproof ☐

Fire Started ☐

Food Inventory

Rations ☐

_____
_____
_____
_____

Water ☐

Hunting ☐

_____
_____
_____

Fishing ☐

_____
_____
_____

Foraging ☐

_____
_____
_____

Journey

Distance Covered

Trail Markers Used

Landmarks Sighted

Animal Prints

Map Sketch

Lat. _____ Long. _____

Party Member	Status	Injuries	Treatment

Date _____

Conditions

Weather

Terrain

Shelter

Shelter Constructed ☐

Type of Shelter

_____

_____

Clothing/Coverings ☐

Waterproof ☐

Animal proof ☐

Sunproof ☐

Fire Started ☐

Map Sketch

Lat. _____ Long. _____

Food Inventory

Rations ☐

_____
_____
_____
_____

Water ☐

Hunting ☐

_____
_____
_____

Fishing ☐

_____
_____
_____

Foraging ☐

_____
_____
_____

Journey

Distance Covered

Trail Markers Used

Landmarks Sighted

Animal Prints

Party Member	Status	Injuries	Treatment

Date _____

Conditions

Weather

Terrain

Shelter

Shelter Constructed ☐

Type of Shelter

_____

_____

_____

Clothing/Coverings ☐
Waterproof ☐
Animal proof ☐
Sunproof ☐
Fire Started ☐

Food Inventory

Rations ☐

_____
_____
_____
_____

Water ☐
Hunting ☐

_____
_____
_____

Fishing ☐

_____
_____
_____

Foraging ☐

_____
_____
_____

Journey

Distance Covered

Trail Markers Used

Landmarks Sighted

Animal Prints

Map Sketch

Lat. _____ Long. _____

Party Member	Status	Injuries	Treatment

Date _____

Conditions

Weather

Terrain

Shelter

Shelter Constructed ☐

Type of Shelter

_____

_____

Clothing/Coverings ☐

Waterproof ☐

Animal proof ☐

Sunproof ☐

Fire Started ☐

Food Inventory

Rations ☐

_____
_____
_____
_____

Water ☐

Hunting ☐

_____
_____
_____

Fishing ☐

_____
_____
_____

Foraging ☐

_____
_____
_____

Journey

Distance Covered

Trail Markers Used

Landmarks Sighted

Animal Prints

Map Sketch

Lat. _____   Long. _____

Party Member	Status	Injuries	Treatment

Date _____

Conditions

Weather

Terrain

Shelter

Shelter Constructed ☐

Type of Shelter

_____

_____

Clothing/Coverings ☐

Waterproof ☐

Animal proof ☐

Sunproof ☐

Fire Started ☐

Food Inventory

Rations ☐

_____
_____
_____
_____

Water ☐

Hunting ☐

_____
_____
_____

Fishing ☐

_____
_____
_____

Foraging ☐

_____
_____

Journey

Distance Covered

Trail Markers Used

Landmarks Sighted

Animal Prints

Map Sketch

Lat. _____   Long. _____

Party Member	Status	Injuries	Treatment

Date _____

Conditions

Weather

Terrain

Shelter

Shelter Constructed ☐

Type of Shelter

_____

_____

Clothing/Coverings ☐

Waterproof ☐

Animal proof ☐

Sunproof ☐

Fire Started ☐

Map Sketch

Lat. _____   Long. _____

Food Inventory

Rations ☐

_____
_____
_____
_____

Water ☐

Hunting ☐

_____
_____
_____

Fishing ☐

_____
_____
_____

Foraging ☐

_____
_____
_____

Journey

Distance Covered

Trail Markers Used

Landmarks Sighted

Animal Prints

Party Member	Status	Injuries	Treatment

Date _____

Conditions

Weather

Terrain

Shelter

Shelter Constructed ☐

Type of Shelter

_____

_____

Clothing/Coverings ☐
Waterproof ☐
Animal proof ☐
Sunproof ☐
Fire Started ☐

Food Inventory

Rations ☐

_____
_____
_____
_____

Water ☐
Hunting ☐

_____
_____
_____

Fishing ☐

_____
_____

Foraging ☐

_____
_____
_____

Map Sketch

Lat.   Long.

Journey

Distance Covered

Trail Markers Used

Landmarks Sighted

Animal Prints

Party Member	Status	Injuries	Treatment

Date _____

Conditions

Weather

Terrain

Shelter

Shelter Constructed ☐

Type of Shelter

_____

_____

_____

Clothing/Coverings ☐
Waterproof ☐
Animal proof ☐
Sunproof ☐
Fire Started ☐

Food Inventory

Rations ☐
_____
_____
_____
_____

Water ☐
Hunting ☐
_____
_____
_____

Fishing ☐
_____
_____

Foraging ☐
_____
_____
_____

Journey

Distance Covered

Trail Markers Used

Landmarks Sighted

Animal Prints

Map Sketch

Lat. _____ Long. _____

Party Member	Status	Injuries	Treatment

Date _____

Conditions

Weather

Terrain

Shelter

Shelter Constructed ☐

Type of Shelter

_____

_____

_____

Clothing/Coverings ☐
Waterproof ☐
Animal proof ☐
Sunproof ☐
Fire Started ☐

Food Inventory

Rations ☐

_____
_____
_____
_____

Water ☐
Hunting ☐

_____
_____
_____

Fishing ☐

_____
_____
_____

Foraging ☐

_____
_____
_____

Journey

Distance Covered

Trail Markers Used

Landmarks Sighted

Animal Prints

Map Sketch

Lat. _____ Long. _____

Party Member	Status	Injuries	Treatment

Date _____

Conditions

Weather

Terrain

Shelter

Shelter Constructed ☐

Type of Shelter

_____

_____

Clothing/Coverings ☐
Waterproof ☐
Animal proof ☐
Sunproof ☐
Fire Started ☐

Food Inventory

Rations ☐

_____
_____
_____
_____

Water ☐
Hunting ☐

_____
_____
_____

Fishing ☐

_____
_____
_____

Foraging ☐

_____
_____
_____

Journey

Distance Covered

Trail Markers Used

Landmarks Sighted

Animal Prints

Map Sketch

Lat. _____ Long. _____

Party Member	Status	Injuries	Treatment

Date _____

Conditions

Weather

Terrain

Food Inventory

Rations ☐

_____
_____
_____
_____

Water ☐
Hunting ☐

_____
_____
_____
_____

Fishing ☐

_____
_____
_____

Foraging ☐

_____
_____
_____

Journey

Distance Covered

Trail Markers Used

Landmarks Sighted

Animal Prints

Shelter

Shelter Constructed ☐

Type of Shelter

_____
_____
_____

Clothing/Coverings ☐
Waterproof ☐
Animal proof ☐
Sunproof ☐
Fire Started ☐

Map Sketch

Lat. _____ Long. _____

Party Member	Status	Injuries	Treatment

Date _____

Conditions

Weather

Terrain

Food Inventory

Rations ☐

_____
_____
_____
_____
_____

Water ☐
Hunting ☐

_____
_____
_____
_____

Fishing ☐

_____
_____
_____

Foraging ☐

_____
_____
_____

Journey

Distance Covered

Trail Markers Used

Landmarks Sighted

Animal Prints

Shelter

Shelter Constructed ☐
Type of Shelter

_____
_____
_____

Clothing/Coverings ☐
Waterproof ☐
Animal proof ☐
Sunproof ☐
Fire Started ☐

Map Sketch

Lat. _____ Long. _____

Party Member	Status	Injuries	Treatment

Date _____

Conditions

Weather

Terrain

Food Inventory

Rations ☐
_____
_____
_____
_____

Water ☐
Hunting ☐
_____
_____
_____

Fishing ☐
_____
_____

Foraging ☐
_____
_____

Journey

Distance Covered

Trail Markers Used

Landmarks Sighted

Animal Prints

Shelter

Shelter Constructed ☐

Type of Shelter
_____
_____
_____

Clothing/Coverings ☐
Waterproof ☐
Animal proof ☐
Sunproof ☐
Fire Started ☐

Map Sketch

Lat. _____ Long. _____

Party Member	Status	Injuries	Treatment

Date _____

Conditions

Weather

Terrain

Shelter

Shelter Constructed ☐

Type of Shelter

_____
_____
_____

Clothing/Coverings ☐
Waterproof ☐
Animal proof ☐
Sunproof ☐
Fire Started ☐

Food Inventory

Rations ☐
_____
_____
_____
_____

Water ☐
Hunting ☐
_____
_____
_____

Fishing ☐
_____
_____
_____

Foraging ☐
_____
_____
_____

Journey

Distance Covered

Trail Markers Used

Landmarks Sighted

Animal Prints

Map Sketch

Lat. _____ Long. _____

Party Member	Status	Injuries	Treatment

Date _____

Conditions

Weather

Terrain

Shelter

Shelter Constructed ☐

Type of Shelter

_____
_____
_____

Clothing/Coverings ☐
Waterproof ☐
Animal proof ☐
Sunproof ☐
Fire Started ☐

Map Sketch

Lat. _____ Long. _____

Food Inventory

Rations ☐
_____
_____
_____
_____

Water ☐
Hunting ☐
_____
_____
_____

Fishing ☐
_____
_____

Foraging ☐
_____
_____

Journey

Distance Covered

Trail Markers Used

Landmarks Sighted

Animal Prints

Party Member	Status	Injuries	Treatment

Date _____

Conditions

Weather

Terrain

Shelter

Shelter Constructed ☐

Type of Shelter

_____

_____

Clothing/Coverings ☐

Waterproof ☐

Animal proof ☐

Sunproof ☐

Fire Started ☐

Food Inventory

Rations ☐

_____
_____
_____
_____

Water ☐

Hunting ☐

_____
_____
_____

Fishing ☐

_____
_____

Foraging ☐

_____
_____
_____
_____

Journey

Distance Covered

Trail Markers Used

Landmarks Sighted

Animal Prints

Map Sketch

Lat. _____ Long. _____

Party Member	Status	Injuries	Treatment

Date _____

Conditions

Weather

Terrain

Shelter

Shelter Constructed ☐

Type of Shelter

_____

_____

Clothing/Coverings ☐
Waterproof ☐
Animal proof ☐
Sunproof ☐
Fire Started ☐

Food Inventory

Rations ☐
_____
_____
_____
_____

Water ☐
Hunting ☐
_____
_____
_____

Fishing ☐
_____
_____

Foraging ☐
_____
_____
_____

Map Sketch

Lat. _____ Long. _____

Journey

Distance Covered

Trail Markers Used

Landmarks Sighted

Animal Prints

Party Member	Status	Injuries	Treatment

Date _____

Conditions

Weather

Terrain

Shelter

Shelter Constructed ☐

Type of Shelter

_____
_____
_____

Clothing/Coverings ☐
Waterproof ☐
Animal proof ☐
Sunproof ☐
Fire Started ☐

Food Inventory

Rations ☐
_____
_____
_____
_____

Water ☐
Hunting ☐
_____
_____
_____

Fishing ☐
_____
_____
_____

Foraging ☐
_____
_____
_____

Journey

Distance Covered

Trail Markers Used

Landmarks Sighted

Animal Prints

Map Sketch

Lat. _____   Long. _____

Party Member	Status	Injuries	Treatment

Date _____

Conditions

Weather

Terrain

Shelter

Shelter Constructed ☐

Type of Shelter

_____

_____

_____

Clothing/Coverings ☐

Waterproof ☐

Animal proof ☐

Sunproof ☐

Fire Started ☐

Food Inventory

Rations ☐

_____
_____
_____
_____

Water ☐

Hunting ☐

_____
_____
_____

Fishing ☐

_____
_____
_____

Foraging ☐

_____
_____
_____

Journey

Distance Covered

Trail Markers Used

Landmarks Sighted

Animal Prints

Map Sketch

Lat. _____   Long. _____

Party Member	Status	Injuries	Treatment

Date _____

Conditions

Weather

Terrain

Shelter

Shelter Constructed ☐

Type of Shelter

_____

_____

Clothing/Coverings ☐

Waterproof ☐

Animal proof ☐

Sunproof ☐

Fire Started ☐

Food Inventory

Rations ☐

_____
_____
_____
_____

Water ☐

Hunting ☐

_____
_____
_____

Fishing ☐

_____
_____
_____

Foraging ☐

_____
_____
_____

Journey

Distance Covered

Trail Markers Used

Landmarks Sighted

Animal Prints

Map Sketch

Lat. _____   Long. _____

Party Member	Status	Injuries	Treatment

Date _____

Conditions

Weather

Terrain

Shelter

Shelter Constructed ☐

Type of Shelter

_____
_____
_____

Clothing/Coverings ☐
Waterproof ☐
Animal proof ☐
Sunproof ☐
Fire Started ☐

Map Sketch

Lat. _____ Long. _____

Food Inventory

Rations ☐
_____
_____
_____
_____

Water ☐
Hunting ☐
_____
_____
_____

Fishing ☐
_____
_____
_____

Foraging ☐
_____
_____
_____

Journey

Distance Covered

Trail Markers Used

Landmarks Sighted

Animal Prints

Party Member	Status	Injuries	Treatment

Date _____

Conditions

Weather

Terrain

Shelter

Shelter Constructed ☐

Type of Shelter

_____

_____

Clothing/Coverings ☐
Waterproof ☐
Animal proof ☐
Sunproof ☐
Fire Started ☐

Food Inventory

Rations ☐
_____
_____
_____
_____

Water ☐
Hunting ☐
_____
_____
_____

Fishing ☐
_____
_____
_____

Foraging ☐
_____
_____
_____

Journey

Distance Covered

Trail Markers Used

Landmarks Sighted

Animal Prints

Map Sketch

Lat. _____ Long. _____

Party Member	Status	Injuries	Treatment

Date _____

Conditions

Weather

Terrain

Shelter

Shelter Constructed ☐

Type of Shelter

_____

_____

_____

Clothing/Coverings ☐
Waterproof ☐
Animal proof ☐
Sunproof ☐
Fire Started ☐

Food Inventory

Rations ☐

_____
_____
_____
_____

Water ☐
Hunting ☐

_____
_____
_____

Fishing ☐

_____
_____

Foraging ☐

_____
_____
_____

Journey

Distance Covered

Trail Markers Used

Landmarks Sighted

Animal Prints

Map Sketch

Lat. _____ Long. _____

Party Member	Status	Injuries	Treatment

Date _____

Conditions

Weather

Terrain

Shelter

Shelter Constructed ☐

Type of Shelter

_____

_____

Clothing/Coverings ☐

Waterproof ☐

Animal proof ☐

Sunproof ☐

Fire Started ☐

Food Inventory

Rations ☐

_____
_____
_____
_____

Water ☐

Hunting ☐

_____
_____
_____

Fishing ☐

_____
_____
_____

Foraging ☐

_____
_____
_____

Journey

Distance Covered

Trail Markers Used

Landmarks Sighted

Animal Prints

Map Sketch

Lat. _____ Long. _____

Party Member	Status	Injuries	Treatment

Date _____

Conditions

Weather

Terrain

Shelter

Shelter Constructed ☐

Type of Shelter

_____

_____

_____

Clothing/Coverings ☐
Waterproof ☐
Animal proof ☐
Sunproof ☐
Fire Started ☐

Food Inventory

Rations ☐
_____
_____
_____
_____

Water ☐
Hunting ☐
_____
_____
_____

Fishing ☐
_____
_____

Foraging ☐
_____
_____

Map Sketch

Lat. _____ Long. _____

Journey

Distance Covered

Trail Markers Used

Landmarks Sighted

Animal Prints

Party Member	Status	Injuries	Treatment

Date _____

Conditions

Weather

Terrain

Shelter

Shelter Constructed ☐

Type of Shelter

_____

_____

Clothing/Coverings ☐
Waterproof ☐
Animal proof ☐
Sunproof ☐
Fire Started ☐

Food Inventory

Rations ☐

_____
_____
_____
_____

Water ☐
Hunting ☐

_____
_____
_____

Fishing ☐

_____
_____
_____

Foraging ☐

_____
_____
_____

Journey

Distance Covered

Trail Markers Used

Landmarks Sighted

Animal Prints

Map Sketch

Lat. _____ Long. _____

Party Member	Status	Injuries	Treatment

Date _____

Conditions

Weather

Terrain

Shelter

Shelter Constructed ☐

Type of Shelter

_____

_____

Clothing/Coverings ☐

Waterproof ☐

Animal proof ☐

Sunproof ☐

Fire Started ☐

Food Inventory

Rations ☐

_____
_____
_____
_____

Water ☐

Hunting ☐

_____
_____
_____

Fishing ☐

_____
_____

Foraging ☐

_____
_____
_____

Journey

Distance Covered

Trail Markers Used

Landmarks Sighted

Animal Prints

Map Sketch

Lat. _____ Long. _____

Party Member	Status	Injuries	Treatment

Date _____

Conditions

Weather

Terrain

Shelter

Shelter Constructed ☐

Type of Shelter

_____

_____

_____

Clothing/Coverings ☐

Waterproof ☐

Animal proof ☐

Sunproof ☐

Fire Started ☐

Food Inventory

Rations ☐

_____
_____
_____
_____
_____

Water ☐

Hunting ☐

_____
_____
_____

Fishing ☐

_____
_____
_____

Foraging ☐

_____
_____
_____

Journey

Distance Covered

Trail Markers Used

Landmarks Sighted

Animal Prints

Map Sketch

Lat. _____   Long. _____

Party Member	Status	Injuries	Treatment

Date _____

Conditions

Weather

Terrain

Shelter

Shelter Constructed ☐

Type of Shelter

_____

_____

Clothing/Coverings ☐

Waterproof ☐

Animal proof ☐

Sunproof ☐

Fire Started ☐

Food Inventory

Rations ☐

_____
_____
_____
_____

Water ☐

Hunting ☐

_____
_____
_____

Fishing ☐

_____
_____

Foraging ☐

_____
_____
_____

Map Sketch

Lat. _____ Long. _____

Journey

Distance Covered

Trail Markers Used

Landmarks Sighted

Animal Prints

Party Member	Status	Injuries	Treatment

Date _____

Conditions

Weather

Terrain

Shelter

Shelter Constructed ☐

Type of Shelter

_____

_____

Clothing/Coverings ☐
Waterproof ☐
Animal proof ☐
Sunproof ☐
Fire Started ☐

Food Inventory

Rations ☐

_____
_____
_____
_____

Water ☐
Hunting ☐

_____
_____
_____

Fishing ☐

_____
_____

Foraging ☐

_____
_____
_____

Journey

Distance Covered

Trail Markers Used

Landmarks Sighted

Animal Prints

Map Sketch

Lat. _____ Long. _____

Party Member	Status	Injuries	Treatment

Date _____

Conditions

Weather

Terrain

Shelter

Shelter Constructed ☐

Type of Shelter

_____
_____
_____

Clothing/Coverings ☐
Waterproof ☐
Animal proof ☐
Sunproof ☐
Fire Started ☐

Map Sketch

Lat. _____ Long. _____

Food Inventory

Rations ☐

_____
_____
_____
_____

Water ☐
Hunting ☐

_____
_____
_____

Fishing ☐

_____
_____
_____

Foraging ☐

_____
_____
_____

Journey

Distance Covered

Trail Markers Used

Landmarks Sighted

Animal Prints

Party Member	Status	Injuries	Treatment

Date _____

Conditions

Weather

Terrain

Shelter

Shelter Constructed ☐

Type of Shelter

_____

_____

Clothing/Coverings ☐
Waterproof ☐
Animal proof ☐
Sunproof ☐
Fire Started ☐

Food Inventory

Rations ☐

_____
_____
_____
_____

Water ☐
Hunting ☐

_____
_____
_____

Fishing ☐

_____
_____
_____

Foraging ☐

_____
_____
_____

Journey

Distance Covered

Trail Markers Used

Landmarks Sighted

Animal Prints

Map Sketch

Lat.   Long.

Party Member	Status	Injuries	Treatment

Date _____

Conditions

Weather

Terrain

Shelter

Shelter Constructed ☐

Type of Shelter

_____

_____

Clothing/Coverings ☐

Waterproof ☐

Animal proof ☐

Sunproof ☐

Fire Started ☐

Food Inventory

Rations ☐

_____
_____
_____
_____

Water ☐

Hunting ☐

_____
_____

Fishing ☐

_____
_____

Foraging ☐

_____
_____

Journey

Distance Covered

Trail Markers Used

Landmarks Sighted

Animal Prints

Map Sketch

Lat. _____ Long. _____

Party Member	Status	Injuries	Treatment

Date _____

Conditions

Weather

Terrain

Food Inventory

Rations ☐
_____
_____
_____
_____

Water ☐
Hunting ☐
_____
_____
_____

Fishing ☐
_____
_____
_____

Foraging ☐
_____
_____
_____

Journey

Distance Covered

Trail Markers Used

Landmarks Sighted

Animal Prints

Shelter

Shelter Constructed ☐

Type of Shelter
_____
_____

Clothing/Coverings ☐
Waterproof ☐
Animal proof ☐
Sunproof ☐
Fire Started ☐

Map Sketch

Lat. _____ Long. _____

Party Member	Status	Injuries	Treatment

Date _____

Conditions

Weather

Terrain

Shelter

Shelter Constructed ☐

Type of Shelter

_____
_____
_____

Clothing/Coverings ☐
Waterproof ☐
Animal proof ☐
Sunproof ☐
Fire Started ☐

Food Inventory

Rations ☐
_____
_____
_____
_____
_____

Water ☐
Hunting ☐
_____
_____
_____

Fishing ☐
_____
_____
_____

Foraging ☐
_____
_____
_____

Journey

Distance Covered

Trail Markers Used

Landmarks Sighted

Animal Prints

Map Sketch

Lat. _____   Long. _____

Party Member	Status	Injuries	Treatment

Date _____

Conditions

Weather

Terrain

Shelter

Shelter Constructed ☐

Type of Shelter

_____
_____
_____

Clothing/Coverings ☐
Waterproof ☐
Animal proof ☐
Sunproof ☐
Fire Started ☐

Food Inventory

Rations ☐
_____
_____
_____
_____

Water ☐
Hunting ☐
_____
_____
_____

Fishing ☐
_____
_____
_____

Foraging ☐
_____
_____
_____

Journey

Distance Covered

Trail Markers Used

Landmarks Sighted

Animal Prints

Map Sketch

Lat. _____ Long. _____

Party Member	Status	Injuries	Treatment

Date _____

Conditions

Weather

Terrain

Shelter

Shelter Constructed ☐

Type of Shelter

_____
_____
_____

Clothing/Coverings ☐
Waterproof ☐
Animal proof ☐
Sunproof ☐
Fire Started ☐

Food Inventory

Rations ☐
_____
_____
_____
_____
_____

Water ☐
Hunting ☐
_____
_____
_____

Fishing ☐
_____
_____
_____

Foraging ☐
_____
_____
_____

Journey

Distance Covered

Trail Markers Used

Landmarks Sighted

Animal Prints

Map Sketch

Lat. _____   Long. _____

Party Member	Status	Injuries	Treatment

Date _____

Conditions

Weather

Terrain

Shelter

Shelter Constructed ☐

Type of Shelter

_____
_____

Clothing/Coverings ☐
Waterproof ☐
Animal proof ☐
Sunproof ☐
Fire Started ☐

Map Sketch

Lat. _____ Long. _____

Food Inventory

Rations ☐
_____
_____
_____
_____

Water ☐
Hunting ☐
_____
_____
_____

Fishing ☐
_____
_____
_____

Foraging ☐
_____
_____

Journey

Distance Covered

Trail Markers Used

Landmarks Sighted

Animal Prints

Party Member	Status	Injuries	Treatment

Date _____

Conditions

Weather

Terrain

Shelter

Shelter Constructed ☐

Type of Shelter

_____

_____

Clothing/Coverings ☐
Waterproof ☐
Animal proof ☐
Sunproof ☐
Fire Started ☐

Food Inventory

Rations ☐
_____
_____
_____
_____

Water ☐
Hunting ☐
_____
_____
_____

Fishing ☐
_____
_____
_____

Foraging ☐
_____
_____
_____

Journey

Distance Covered

Trail Markers Used

Landmarks Sighted

Animal Prints

Map Sketch

Lat. _____ Long. _____

Party Member	Status	Injuries	Treatment

Date _____

Conditions

Weather

Terrain

Shelter

Shelter Constructed ☐

Type of Shelter

_____

_____

_____

Clothing/Coverings ☐

Waterproof ☐

Animal proof ☐

Sunproof ☐

Fire Started ☐

Map Sketch

Lat. _____ Long. _____

Food Inventory

Rations ☐

_____
_____
_____
_____
_____

Water ☐

Hunting ☐

_____
_____
_____
_____

Fishing ☐

_____
_____
_____

Foraging ☐

_____
_____
_____

Journey

Distance Covered

Trail Markers Used

Landmarks Sighted

Animal Prints

Party Member	Status	Injuries	Treatment

Date _____

Conditions

Weather

Terrain

Shelter

Shelter Constructed ☐

Type of Shelter

_____

_____

Clothing/Coverings ☐
Waterproof ☐
Animal proof ☐
Sunproof ☐
Fire Started ☐

Map Sketch

Lat. _____ Long. _____

Food Inventory

Rations ☐
_____
_____
_____
_____

Water ☐
Hunting ☐
_____
_____
_____

Fishing ☐
_____
_____

Foraging ☐
_____
_____

Journey

Distance Covered

Trail Markers Used

Landmarks Sighted

Animal Prints

Party Member	Status	Injuries	Treatment

Date _____

Conditions

Weather

Terrain

Shelter

Shelter Constructed ☐

Type of Shelter

_____

_____

Clothing/Coverings ☐
Waterproof ☐
Animal proof ☐
Sunproof ☐
Fire Started ☐

Map Sketch

Lat. _____ Long. _____

Food Inventory

Rations ☐
_____
_____
_____
_____

Water ☐
Hunting ☐
_____
_____
_____

Fishing ☐
_____
_____

Foraging ☐
_____
_____

Journey

Distance Covered

Trail Markers Used

Landmarks Sighted

Animal Prints

Party Member	Status	Injuries	Treatment

Date _____

Conditions

Weather

Terrain

Shelter

Shelter Constructed ☐

Type of Shelter

_____

_____

Clothing/Coverings ☐

Waterproof ☐

Animal proof ☐

Sunproof ☐

Fire Started ☐

Food Inventory

Rations ☐

_____
_____
_____
_____

Water ☐

Hunting ☐

_____
_____
_____

Fishing ☐

_____
_____
_____

Foraging ☐

_____
_____
_____

Journey

Distance Covered

Trail Markers Used

Landmarks Sighted

Animal Prints

Map Sketch

Lat. _____ Long. _____

Party Member	Status	Injuries	Treatment

Date _____

Conditions

Weather

Terrain

Shelter

Shelter Constructed ☐

Type of Shelter

_____

_____

_____

Clothing/Coverings ☐
Waterproof ☐
Animal proof ☐
Sunproof ☐
Fire Started ☐

Food Inventory

Rations ☐

_____
_____
_____
_____
_____

Water ☐
Hunting ☐

_____
_____
_____

Fishing ☐

_____
_____
_____

Foraging ☐

_____
_____
_____

Journey

Distance Covered

Trail Markers Used

Landmarks Sighted

Animal Prints

Map Sketch

Lat. _____ Long. _____

Party Member	Status	Injuries	Treatment

Date _____

Conditions

Weather

Terrain

Shelter

Shelter Constructed ☐

Type of Shelter

_____

_____

_____

Clothing/Coverings ☐
Waterproof ☐
Animal proof ☐
Sunproof ☐
Fire Started ☐

Food Inventory

Rations ☐
_____
_____
_____
_____

Water ☐
Hunting ☐
_____
_____
_____

Fishing ☐
_____
_____

Foraging ☐
_____
_____

Journey

Distance Covered

Trail Markers Used

Landmarks Sighted

Animal Prints

Map Sketch

Lat. _____ Long. _____

Party Member	Status	Injuries	Treatment

Date _____

Conditions

Weather

Terrain

Shelter

Shelter Constructed ☐

Type of Shelter

_____

_____

Clothing/Coverings ☐

Waterproof ☐

Animal proof ☐

Sunproof ☐

Fire Started ☐

Food Inventory

Rations ☐

_____
_____
_____
_____

Water ☐

Hunting ☐

_____
_____
_____

Fishing ☐

_____
_____
_____

Foraging ☐

_____
_____
_____

Journey

Distance Covered

Trail Markers Used

Landmarks Sighted

Animal Prints

Map Sketch

Lat. _____ Long. _____

Party Member	Status	Injuries	Treatment

Date _____

Conditions

Weather

Terrain

Shelter

Shelter Constructed ☐

Type of Shelter

_____

_____

Clothing/Coverings ☐
Waterproof ☐
Animal proof ☐
Sunproof ☐
Fire Started ☐

Food Inventory

Rations ☐

_____
_____
_____
_____

Water ☐
Hunting ☐

_____
_____
_____

Fishing ☐

_____
_____

Foraging ☐

_____
_____
_____

Journey

Distance Covered

Trail Markers Used

Landmarks Sighted

Animal Prints

Map Sketch

Lat. _____ Long. _____

Party Member	Status	Injuries	Treatment

Date _____

Conditions

Weather

Terrain

Shelter

Shelter Constructed ☐

Type of Shelter

_____

_____

_____

Clothing/Coverings ☐
Waterproof ☐
Animal proof ☐
Sunproof ☐
Fire Started ☐

Food Inventory

Rations ☐

_____
_____
_____
_____

Water ☐
Hunting ☐

_____
_____
_____

Fishing ☐

_____
_____
_____

Foraging ☐

_____
_____

Journey

Distance Covered

Trail Markers Used

Landmarks Sighted

Animal Prints

Map Sketch

Lat. _____ Long. _____

Party Member	Status	Injuries	Treatment

Date _____

Conditions

Weather

Terrain

Shelter

Shelter Constructed ☐

Type of Shelter

_____

_____

Clothing/Coverings ☐
Waterproof ☐
Animal proof ☐
Sunproof ☐
Fire Started ☐

Map Sketch

Lat. _____ Long. _____

Food Inventory

Rations ☐
_____
_____
_____
_____

Water ☐
Hunting ☐
_____
_____
_____

Fishing ☐
_____
_____
_____

Foraging ☐
_____
_____
_____

Journey

Distance Covered

Trail Markers Used

Landmarks Sighted

Animal Prints

Party Member	Status	Injuries	Treatment

Date _____

Conditions

Weather

Terrain

Shelter

Shelter Constructed ☐

Type of Shelter
_____
_____

Clothing/Coverings ☐
Waterproof ☐
Animal proof ☐
Sunproof ☐
Fire Started ☐

Food Inventory

Rations ☐
_____
_____
_____
_____

Water ☐
Hunting ☐
_____
_____
_____

Fishing ☐
_____
_____
_____

Foraging ☐
_____
_____
_____

Journey

Distance Covered

Trail Markers Used

Landmarks Sighted

Animal Prints

Map Sketch

Lat. _____ Long. _____

Party Member	Status	Injuries	Treatment

Date _____

Conditions

Weather

Terrain

Shelter

Shelter Constructed ☐

Type of Shelter

_____

_____

_____

Clothing/Coverings ☐
Waterproof ☐
Animal proof ☐
Sunproof ☐
Fire Started ☐

Map Sketch

Lat. _____   Long. _____

Food Inventory

Rations ☐
_____
_____
_____
_____

Water ☐
Hunting ☐
_____
_____
_____

Fishing ☐
_____
_____

Foraging ☐
_____
_____

Journey

Distance Covered

Trail Markers Used

Landmarks Sighted

Animal Prints

Party Member	Status	Injuries	Treatment

Date _____

Conditions

Weather

Terrain

Shelter

Shelter Constructed ☐

Type of Shelter

_____

_____

_____

Clothing/Coverings ☐
Waterproof ☐
Animal proof ☐
Sunproof ☐
Fire Started ☐

Food Inventory

Rations ☐

_____
_____
_____
_____
_____

Water ☐

Hunting ☐

_____
_____
_____
_____

Fishing ☐

_____
_____
_____

Foraging ☐

_____
_____
_____
_____

Journey

Distance Covered

Trail Markers Used

Landmarks Sighted

Animal Prints

Map Sketch

Lat. _____   Long. _____

Party Member	Status	Injuries	Treatment

Date _____

Conditions

Weather

Terrain

Shelter

Shelter Constructed ☐

Type of Shelter

_____

_____

Clothing/Coverings ☐
Waterproof ☐
Animal proof ☐
Sunproof ☐
Fire Started ☐

Food Inventory

Rations ☐
_____
_____
_____
_____
_____

Water ☐
Hunting ☐
_____
_____
_____

Fishing ☐
_____
_____
_____

Foraging ☐
_____
_____
_____

Journey

Distance Covered

Trail Markers Used

Landmarks Sighted

Animal Prints

Map Sketch

Lat. _____ Long. _____

Party Member	Status	Injuries	Treatment

Date _____

Conditions

Weather

Terrain

Shelter

Shelter Constructed ☐
Type of Shelter

_____
_____
_____

Clothing/Coverings ☐
Waterproof ☐
Animal proof ☐
Sunproof ☐
Fire Started ☐

Food Inventory

Rations ☐
_____
_____
_____
_____

Water ☐
Hunting ☐
_____
_____
_____

Fishing ☐
_____
_____
_____

Foraging ☐
_____
_____
_____

Journey

Distance Covered

Trail Markers Used

Landmarks Sighted

Animal Prints

Map Sketch

Lat. _____ Long. _____

Party Member	Status	Injuries	Treatment

Date _____

Conditions

Weather

Terrain

Shelter

Shelter Constructed ☐

Type of Shelter

_____

_____

Clothing/Coverings ☐
Waterproof ☐
Animal proof ☐
Sunproof ☐
Fire Started ☐

Food Inventory

Rations ☐

_____
_____
_____
_____

Water ☐
Hunting ☐

_____
_____
_____

Fishing ☐

_____
_____
_____

Foraging ☐

_____
_____
_____

Journey

Distance Covered

Trail Markers Used

Landmarks Sighted

Animal Prints

Map Sketch

Lat. _____ Long. _____

Party Member	Status	Injuries	Treatment

Date _____

Conditions

Weather

Terrain

Food Inventory

Rations ☐

_____
_____
_____
_____

Water ☐

Hunting ☐

_____
_____
_____

Fishing ☐

_____
_____
_____

Foraging ☐

_____
_____
_____

Journey

Distance Covered

Trail Markers Used

Landmarks Sighted

Animal Prints

Shelter

Shelter Constructed ☐

Type of Shelter

_____
_____
_____

Clothing/Coverings ☐

Waterproof ☐

Animal proof ☐

Sunproof ☐

Fire Started ☐

Map Sketch

Lat. _____   Long. _____

Party Member	Status	Injuries	Treatment

Date _____

Conditions

Weather

Terrain

Shelter

Shelter Constructed ☐

Type of Shelter
_____
_____
_____

Clothing/Coverings ☐
Waterproof ☐
Animal proof ☐
Sunproof ☐
Fire Started ☐

Map Sketch

Lat. _____ Long. _____

Food Inventory

Rations ☐
_____
_____
_____
_____

Water ☐
Hunting ☐
_____
_____
_____

Fishing ☐
_____
_____
_____

Foraging ☐
_____
_____
_____

Journey

Distance Covered

Trail Markers Used

Landmarks Sighted

Animal Prints

Party Member	Status	Injuries	Treatment

Date _____

Conditions

Weather

Terrain

Shelter

Shelter Constructed ☐

Type of Shelter

_____

_____

_____

Clothing/Coverings ☐
Waterproof ☐
Animal proof ☐
Sunproof ☐
Fire Started ☐

Food Inventory

Rations ☐

_____
_____
_____
_____

Water ☐
Hunting ☐

_____
_____
_____

Fishing ☐

_____
_____
_____

Foraging ☐

_____
_____
_____

Journey

Distance Covered

Trail Markers Used

Landmarks Sighted

Animal Prints

Map Sketch

Lat. _____ Long. _____

Party Member	Status	Injuries	Treatment

Date _____

Conditions

Weather

Terrain

Shelter

Shelter Constructed ☐

Type of Shelter

_____

_____

Clothing/Coverings ☐
Waterproof ☐
Animal proof ☐
Sunproof ☐
Fire Started ☐

Food Inventory

Rations ☐

_____
_____
_____
_____

Water ☐
Hunting ☐

_____
_____
_____

Fishing ☐

_____
_____

Foraging ☐

_____
_____

Journey

Distance Covered

Trail Markers Used

Landmarks Sighted

Animal Prints

Map Sketch

Lat. _____ Long. _____

Party Member	Status	Injuries	Treatment

Date _____

Conditions

Weather

Terrain

Shelter

Shelter Constructed ☐

Type of Shelter

_____

_____

Clothing/Coverings ☐

Waterproof ☐

Animal proof ☐

Sunproof ☐

Fire Started ☐

Food Inventory

Rations ☐

_____
_____
_____
_____

Water ☐

Hunting ☐

_____
_____
_____

Fishing ☐

_____
_____
_____

Foraging ☐

_____
_____
_____

Journey

Distance Covered

Trail Markers Used

Landmarks Sighted

Animal Prints

Map Sketch

Lat. _____   Long. _____

Party Member	Status	Injuries	Treatment

Date _____

Conditions

Weather

Terrain

Shelter

Shelter Constructed ☐

Type of Shelter

_____

_____

Clothing/Coverings ☐
Waterproof ☐
Animal proof ☐
Sunproof ☐
Fire Started ☐

Food Inventory

Rations ☐
_____
_____
_____
_____

Water ☐
Hunting ☐
_____
_____
_____

Fishing ☐
_____
_____

Foraging ☐
_____
_____

Map Sketch

Lat. _____ Long. _____

Journey

Distance Covered

Trail Markers Used

Landmarks Sighted

Animal Prints

Party Member	Status	Injuries	Treatment

Date _____

Conditions

Weather

Terrain

Shelter

Shelter Constructed ☐

Type of Shelter

_____
_____
_____

Clothing/Coverings ☐
Waterproof ☐
Animal proof ☐
Sunproof ☐
Fire Started ☐

Food Inventory

Rations ☐
_____
_____
_____
_____

Water ☐
Hunting ☐
_____
_____
_____

Fishing ☐
_____
_____

Foraging ☐
_____
_____
_____

Journey

Distance Covered

Trail Markers Used

Landmarks Sighted

Animal Prints

Map Sketch

Lat. _____ Long. _____

Party Member	Status	Injuries	Treatment

Date _____

Conditions

Weather

Terrain

Shelter

Shelter Constructed ☐

Type of Shelter

_____

_____

_____

Clothing/Coverings ☐
Waterproof ☐
Animal proof ☐
Sunproof ☐
Fire Started ☐

Food Inventory

Rations ☐

_____
_____
_____
_____

Water ☐
Hunting ☐

_____
_____
_____

Fishing ☐

_____
_____
_____

Foraging ☐

_____
_____
_____

Journey

Distance Covered

Trail Markers Used

Landmarks Sighted

Animal Prints

Map Sketch

Lat. _____ Long. _____

Party Member	Status	Injuries	Treatment

Date _____

Conditions

Weather

Terrain

Shelter

Shelter Constructed ☐

Type of Shelter

_____

_____

Clothing/Coverings ☐
Waterproof ☐
Animal proof ☐
Sunproof ☐
Fire Started ☐

Food Inventory

Rations ☐
_____
_____
_____
_____

Water ☐
Hunting ☐
_____
_____
_____

Fishing ☐
_____
_____

Foraging ☐
_____
_____

Journey

Distance Covered

Trail Markers Used

Landmarks Sighted

Animal Prints

Map Sketch

Lat. _____ Long. _____

Party Member	Status	Injuries	Treatment

Date _____

Conditions

Weather

Terrain

Food Inventory

Rations ☐
_____
_____
_____
_____

Water ☐
Hunting ☐
_____
_____
_____

Fishing ☐
_____
_____
_____

Foraging ☐
_____
_____

Journey

Distance Covered

Trail Markers Used

Landmarks Sighted

Animal Prints

Shelter

Shelter Constructed ☐

Type of Shelter
_____
_____

Clothing/Coverings ☐
Waterproof ☐
Animal proof ☐
Sunproof ☐
Fire Started ☐

Map Sketch

Lat. _____ Long. _____

Party Member	Status	Injuries	Treatment

Date _____

Conditions

Weather

Terrain

Shelter

Shelter Constructed ☐

Type of Shelter

_____

_____

Clothing/Coverings ☐

Waterproof ☐

Animal proof ☐

Sunproof ☐

Fire Started ☐

Food Inventory

Rations ☐

_____
_____
_____
_____

Water ☐

Hunting ☐

_____
_____
_____

Fishing ☐

_____
_____
_____

Foraging ☐

_____
_____

Map Sketch

Lat. _____ Long. _____

Journey

Distance Covered

Trail Markers Used

Landmarks Sighted

Animal Prints

Party Member	Status	Injuries	Treatment

Date _____

Conditions

Weather

Terrain

Shelter

Shelter Constructed ☐

Type of Shelter

_____
_____
_____

Clothing/Coverings ☐
Waterproof ☐
Animal proof ☐
Sunproof ☐
Fire Started ☐

Food Inventory

Rations ☐
_____
_____
_____
_____

Water ☐
Hunting ☐
_____
_____
_____

Fishing ☐
_____
_____
_____

Foraging ☐
_____
_____

Journey

Distance Covered

Trail Markers Used

Landmarks Sighted

Animal Prints

Map Sketch

Lat. _____ Long. _____

Party Member	Status	Injuries	Treatment

Date _____

Conditions

Weather

Terrain

Shelter

Shelter Constructed ☐

Type of Shelter

_____

_____

_____

Clothing/Coverings ☐

Waterproof ☐

Animal proof ☐

Sunproof ☐

Fire Started ☐

Map Sketch

Lat. _____ Long. _____

Food Inventory

Rations ☐

_____
_____
_____
_____

Water ☐

Hunting ☐

_____
_____
_____

Fishing ☐

_____
_____
_____

Foraging ☐

_____
_____
_____

Journey

Distance Covered

Trail Markers Used

Landmarks Sighted

Animal Prints

Party Member	Status	Injuries	Treatment

Date _____

Conditions

Weather

Terrain

Shelter

Shelter Constructed ☐

Type of Shelter

_____

_____

Clothing/Coverings ☐

Waterproof ☐

Animal proof ☐

Sunproof ☐

Fire Started ☐

Food Inventory

Rations ☐

_____
_____
_____
_____

Water ☐

Hunting ☐

_____
_____
_____

Fishing ☐

_____
_____
_____

Foraging ☐

_____
_____

Journey

Distance Covered

Trail Markers Used

Landmarks Sighted

Animal Prints

Map Sketch

Lat. _____ Long. _____

Party Member	Status	Injuries	Treatment

Date _____

Conditions

Weather

Terrain

Shelter

Shelter Constructed ☐
Type of Shelter

_____

_____

Clothing/Coverings ☐
Waterproof ☐
Animal proof ☐
Sunproof ☐
Fire Started ☐

Map Sketch

Lat.   Long.

Food Inventory

Rations ☐

_____
_____
_____
_____

Water ☐
Hunting ☐

_____
_____
_____
_____

Fishing ☐

_____
_____
_____

Foraging ☐

_____
_____
_____

Journey

Distance Covered

Trail Markers Used

Landmarks Sighted

Animal Prints

Party Member	Status	Injuries	Treatment

Date _____

Conditions

Weather

Terrain

Shelter

Shelter Constructed ☐

Type of Shelter

_____

_____

_____

Clothing/Coverings ☐

Waterproof ☐

Animal proof ☐

Sunproof ☐

Fire Started ☐

Map Sketch

Lat. _____ Long. _____

Food Inventory

Rations ☐
_____
_____
_____
_____

Water ☐

Hunting ☐
_____
_____
_____

Fishing ☐
_____
_____

Foraging ☐
_____
_____
_____

Journey

Distance Covered

Trail Markers Used

Landmarks Sighted

Animal Prints

Party Member	Status	Injuries	Treatment

Date _____

Conditions

Weather

Terrain

Shelter

Shelter Constructed ☐

Type of Shelter

_____

_____

Clothing/Coverings ☐

Waterproof ☐

Animal proof ☐

Sunproof ☐

Fire Started ☐

Food Inventory

Rations ☐

_____
_____
_____
_____

Water ☐

Hunting ☐

_____
_____
_____

Fishing ☐

_____
_____
_____

Foraging ☐

_____
_____
_____

Journey

Distance Covered

Trail Markers Used

Landmarks Sighted

Animal Prints

Map Sketch

Lat. _____ Long. _____

Party Member	Status	Injuries	Treatment

Date _____

Conditions

Weather

Terrain

Shelter

Shelter Constructed ☐

Type of Shelter

_____

_____

_____

Clothing/Coverings ☐

Waterproof ☐

Animal proof ☐

Sunproof ☐

Fire Started ☐

Food Inventory

Rations ☐

_____
_____
_____
_____

Water ☐

Hunting ☐

_____
_____
_____

Fishing ☐

_____
_____
_____

Foraging ☐

_____
_____
_____

Journey

Distance Covered

Trail Markers Used

Landmarks Sighted

Animal Prints

Map Sketch

Lat.   Long.

Party Member	Status	Injuries	Treatment

Date _____

Conditions

Weather

Terrain

Food Inventory

Rations ☐

_____
_____
_____
_____

Water ☐
Hunting ☐

_____
_____
_____

Fishing ☐

_____
_____

Foraging ☐

_____
_____

Journey

Distance Covered

Trail Markers Used

Landmarks Sighted

Animal Prints

Shelter

Shelter Constructed ☐
Type of Shelter

_____
_____

Clothing/Coverings ☐
Waterproof ☐
Animal proof ☐
Sunproof ☐
Fire Started ☐

Map Sketch

Lat. _____   Long. _____

Party Member	Status	Injuries	Treatment

Date _____

Conditions

Weather

Terrain

Shelter

Shelter Constructed ☐

Type of Shelter

_____

_____

Clothing/Coverings ☐

Waterproof ☐

Animal proof ☐

Sunproof ☐

Fire Started ☐

Map Sketch

Lat. _____ Long. _____

Food Inventory

Rations ☐

_____
_____
_____
_____

Water ☐

Hunting ☐

_____
_____
_____

Fishing ☐

_____
_____

Foraging ☐

_____
_____

Journey

Distance Covered

Trail Markers Used

Landmarks Sighted

Animal Prints

Party Member	Status	Injuries	Treatment

Date _____

Conditions

Weather

Terrain

Shelter

Shelter Constructed ☐

Type of Shelter

_____

_____

_____

Clothing/Coverings ☐
Waterproof ☐
Animal proof ☐
Sunproof ☐
Fire Started ☐

Food Inventory

Rations ☐
_____
_____
_____
_____
_____

Water ☐
Hunting ☐
_____
_____
_____
_____

Fishing ☐
_____
_____
_____

Foraging ☐
_____
_____
_____
_____

Journey

Distance Covered

Trail Markers Used

Landmarks Sighted

Animal Prints

Map Sketch

Lat. _____ Long. _____

Party Member	Status	Injuries	Treatment

Date _____

Conditions

Weather

Terrain

Shelter

Shelter Constructed ☐

Type of Shelter

_____

_____

Clothing/Coverings ☐
Waterproof ☐
Animal proof ☐
Sunproof ☐
Fire Started ☐

Food Inventory

Rations ☐

_____
_____
_____
_____

Water ☐
Hunting ☐

_____
_____
_____

Fishing ☐

_____
_____

Foraging ☐

_____
_____
_____

Journey

Distance Covered

Trail Markers Used

Landmarks Sighted

Animal Prints

Map Sketch

Lat. _____ Long. _____

Party Member	Status	Injuries	Treatment

Date _____

Conditions

Weather

Terrain

Shelter

Shelter Constructed ☐

Type of Shelter

_____

_____

Clothing/Coverings ☐

Waterproof ☐

Animal proof ☐

Sunproof ☐

Fire Started ☐

Food Inventory

Rations ☐

_____
_____
_____
_____

Water ☐
Hunting ☐

_____
_____

Fishing ☐

_____
_____

Foraging ☐

_____
_____

Journey

Distance Covered

Trail Markers Used

Landmarks Sighted

Animal Prints

Map Sketch

Lat. _____ Long. _____

Party Member	Status	Injuries	Treatment

Date _____

Conditions

Weather

Terrain

Shelter

Shelter Constructed ☐

Type of Shelter

_____

_____

Clothing/Coverings ☐

Waterproof ☐

Animal proof ☐

Sunproof ☐

Fire Started ☐

Food Inventory

Rations ☐

_____

_____

_____

_____

Water ☐

Hunting ☐

_____

_____

_____

Fishing ☐

_____

_____

_____

Foraging ☐

_____

_____

_____

Journey

Distance Covered

Trail Markers Used

Landmarks Sighted

Animal Prints

Map Sketch

Lat. _____   Long. _____

Party Member	Status	Injuries	Treatment

Date _____

Conditions

Weather

Terrain

Shelter

Shelter Constructed ☐

Type of Shelter

_____

_____

Clothing/Coverings ☐

Waterproof ☐

Animal proof ☐

Sunproof ☐

Fire Started ☐

Map Sketch

Lat. _____ Long. _____

Food Inventory

Rations ☐

_____
_____
_____
_____

Water ☐
Hunting ☐

_____
_____
_____

Fishing ☐

_____
_____
_____

Foraging ☐

_____
_____
_____

Journey

Distance Covered

Trail Markers Used

Landmarks Sighted

Animal Prints

Party Member	Status	Injuries	Treatment

Date _____

Conditions

Weather

Terrain

Shelter

Shelter Constructed ☐

Type of Shelter
_____
_____

Clothing/Coverings ☐
Waterproof ☐
Animal proof ☐
Sunproof ☐
Fire Started ☐

Food Inventory

Rations ☐
_____
_____
_____
_____

Water ☐
Hunting ☐
_____
_____
_____

Fishing ☐
_____
_____
_____

Foraging ☐
_____
_____
_____

Map Sketch

Lat. _____   Long. _____

Journey

Distance Covered

Trail Markers Used

Landmarks Sighted

Animal Prints

Party Member	Status	Injuries	Treatment

Date _____

Conditions

Weather

Terrain

Shelter

Shelter Constructed ☐

Type of Shelter
_____
_____

Clothing/Coverings ☐
Waterproof ☐
Animal proof ☐
Sunproof ☐
Fire Started ☐

Food Inventory

Rations ☐
_____
_____
_____
_____

Water ☐
Hunting ☐
_____
_____
_____

Fishing ☐
_____
_____
_____

Foraging ☐
_____
_____
_____

Journey

Distance Covered

Trail Markers Used

Landmarks Sighted

Animal Prints

Map Sketch

Lat. _____ Long. _____

Party Member	Status	Injuries	Treatment

Date _____

Conditions

Weather

Terrain

Shelter

Shelter Constructed ☐

Type of Shelter

_____

_____

_____

Clothing/Coverings ☐
Waterproof ☐
Animal proof ☐
Sunproof ☐
Fire Started ☐

Food Inventory

Rations ☐

_____
_____
_____
_____

Water ☐
Hunting ☐

_____
_____
_____
_____

Fishing ☐

_____
_____
_____

Foraging ☐

_____
_____
_____
_____

Map Sketch

Lat. _____ Long. _____

Journey

Distance Covered

Trail Markers Used

Landmarks Sighted

Animal Prints

Party Member	Status	Injuries	Treatment

Date _____

Conditions

Weather

Terrain

Shelter

Shelter Constructed ☐

Type of Shelter

_____

_____

_____

Clothing/Coverings ☐

Waterproof ☐

Animal proof ☐

Sunproof ☐

Fire Started ☐

Food Inventory

Rations ☐

_____
_____
_____
_____

Water ☐
Hunting ☐

_____
_____
_____

Fishing ☐

_____
_____
_____

Foraging ☐

_____
_____
_____

Journey

Distance Covered

Trail Markers Used

Landmarks Sighted

Animal Prints

Map Sketch

Lat. _____ Long. _____

Party Member	Status	Injuries	Treatment

Date _____

Conditions

Weather

Terrain

Shelter

Shelter Constructed ☐

Type of Shelter

_____

_____

Clothing/Coverings ☐
Waterproof ☐
Animal proof ☐
Sunproof ☐
Fire Started ☐

Food Inventory

Rations ☐

_____
_____
_____
_____

Water ☐
Hunting ☐

_____
_____
_____

Fishing ☐

_____
_____
_____

Foraging ☐

_____
_____
_____

Journey

Distance Covered

Trail Markers Used

Landmarks Sighted

Animal Prints

Map Sketch

Lat. _____   Long. _____

Party Member	Status	Injuries	Treatment

Date _____

Conditions

Weather

Terrain

Shelter

Shelter Constructed ☐

Type of Shelter

_____

_____

Clothing/Coverings ☐
Waterproof ☐
Animal proof ☐
Sunproof ☐
Fire Started ☐

Food Inventory

Rations ☐
_____
_____
_____
_____

Water ☐
Hunting ☐
_____
_____
_____

Fishing ☐
_____
_____
_____

Foraging ☐
_____
_____

Journey

Distance Covered

Trail Markers Used

Landmarks Sighted

Animal Prints

Map Sketch

Lat. _____   Long. _____

Party Member	Status	Injuries	Treatment

Date _____

Conditions

Weather

Terrain

Food Inventory

Rations ☐
_____
_____
_____
_____
_____

Water ☐
Hunting ☐
_____
_____
_____

Fishing ☐
_____
_____

Foraging ☐
_____
_____
_____

Journey

Distance Covered

Trail Markers Used

Landmarks Sighted

Animal Prints

Shelter

Shelter Constructed ☐
Type of Shelter
_____
_____
_____

Clothing/Coverings ☐
Waterproof ☐
Animal proof ☐
Sunproof ☐
Fire Started ☐

Map Sketch

Lat. _____ Long. _____

Party Member	Status	Injuries	Treatment

Date _____

Conditions

Weather

Terrain

Shelter

Shelter Constructed ☐

Type of Shelter

_____

_____

Clothing/Coverings ☐

Waterproof ☐

Animal proof ☐

Sunproof ☐

Fire Started ☐

Map Sketch

Lat. ____   Long. ____

Food Inventory

Rations ☐

_____
_____
_____
_____

Water ☐

Hunting ☐

_____
_____
_____

Fishing ☐

_____
_____
_____

Foraging ☐

_____
_____
_____

Journey

Distance Covered

Trail Markers Used

Landmarks Sighted

Animal Prints

Party Member	Status	Injuries	Treatment

Date _____

Conditions

Weather

Terrain

Shelter

Shelter Constructed ☐

Type of Shelter

_____

_____

Clothing/Coverings ☐
Waterproof ☐
Animal proof ☐
Sunproof ☐
Fire Started ☐

Food Inventory

Rations ☐

_____
_____
_____
_____

Water ☐
Hunting ☐

_____
_____

Fishing ☐

_____
_____

Foraging ☐

_____
_____

Journey

Distance Covered

Trail Markers Used

Landmarks Sighted

Animal Prints

Map Sketch

Lat. _____ Long. _____

Party Member	Status	Injuries	Treatment

Date _____

Conditions

Weather

Terrain

Shelter

Shelter Constructed ☐

Type of Shelter

_____

_____

Clothing/Coverings ☐
Waterproof ☐
Animal proof ☐
Sunproof ☐
Fire Started ☐

Food Inventory

Rations ☐

_____
_____
_____
_____

Water ☐
Hunting ☐

_____
_____
_____

Fishing ☐

_____
_____
_____

Foraging ☐

_____
_____

Journey

Distance Covered

Trail Markers Used

Landmarks Sighted

Animal Prints

Map Sketch

Lat. _____ Long. _____

Party Member	Status	Injuries	Treatment

Date _____

Conditions

Weather

Terrain

Shelter

Shelter Constructed ☐

Type of Shelter

_____
_____
_____

Clothing/Coverings ☐
Waterproof ☐
Animal proof ☐
Sunproof ☐
Fire Started ☐

Food Inventory

Rations ☐
_____
_____
_____
_____

Water ☐
Hunting ☐
_____
_____
_____
_____

Fishing ☐
_____
_____
_____

Foraging ☐
_____
_____
_____

Journey

Distance Covered

Trail Markers Used

Landmarks Sighted

Animal Prints

Map Sketch

Lat. _____ Long. _____

Party Member	Status	Injuries	Treatment

Date _____

Conditions

Weather

Terrain

Shelter

Shelter Constructed ☐

Type of Shelter

_____

_____

Clothing/Coverings ☐

Waterproof ☐

Animal proof ☐

Sunproof ☐

Fire Started ☐

Food Inventory

Rations ☐

_____
_____
_____
_____
_____

Water ☐

Hunting ☐

_____
_____
_____

Fishing ☐

_____
_____
_____

Foraging ☐

_____
_____
_____

Journey

Distance Covered

Trail Markers Used

Landmarks Sighted

Animal Prints

Map Sketch

Lat. _____ Long. _____

Party Member	Status	Injuries	Treatment

Date _____

Conditions

Weather

Terrain

Shelter

Shelter Constructed ☐
Type of Shelter
_____
_____

Clothing/Coverings ☐
Waterproof ☐
Animal proof ☐
Sunproof ☐
Fire Started ☐

Food Inventory

Rations ☐
_____
_____
_____
_____

Water ☐
Hunting ☐
_____
_____
_____

Fishing ☐
_____
_____

Foraging ☐
_____
_____
_____

Journey

Distance Covered

Trail Markers Used

Landmarks Sighted

Animal Prints

Map Sketch

Lat. _____ Long. _____

Party Member	Status	Injuries	Treatment

Date _____

Conditions

Weather

Terrain

Shelter

Shelter Constructed ☐

Type of Shelter

_____
_____
_____

Clothing/Coverings ☐
Waterproof ☐
Animal proof ☐
Sunproof ☐
Fire Started ☐

Food Inventory

Rations ☐
_____
_____
_____
_____

Water ☐
Hunting ☐
_____
_____
_____

Fishing ☐
_____
_____

Foraging ☐
_____
_____
_____

Journey

Distance Covered

Trail Markers Used

Landmarks Sighted

Animal Prints

Map Sketch

Lat. _____ Long. _____

Party Member	Status	Injuries	Treatment

Date _____

Conditions

Weather

Terrain

Shelter

Shelter Constructed ☐

Type of Shelter

_____

_____

_____

Clothing/Coverings ☐
Waterproof ☐
Animal proof ☐
Sunproof ☐
Fire Started ☐

Food Inventory

Rations ☐
_____
_____
_____
_____

Water ☐
Hunting ☐
_____
_____
_____

Fishing ☐
_____
_____
_____

Foraging ☐
_____
_____
_____

Journey

Distance Covered

Trail Markers Used

Landmarks Sighted

Animal Prints

Map Sketch

Lat. _____ Long. _____

Party Member	Status	Injuries	Treatment

Date _____

Conditions

Weather

Terrain

Shelter

Shelter Constructed ☐

Type of Shelter

_____
_____
_____

Clothing/Coverings ☐
Waterproof ☐
Animal proof ☐
Sunproof ☐
Fire Started ☐

Map Sketch

Lat. _____   Long. _____

Food Inventory

Rations ☐
_____
_____
_____
_____
_____

Water ☐
Hunting ☐
_____
_____
_____
_____

Fishing ☐
_____
_____
_____
_____

Foraging ☐
_____
_____
_____
_____

Journey

Distance Covered

Trail Markers Used

Landmarks Sighted

Animal Prints

Party Member	Status	Injuries	Treatment

Date _____

Conditions

Weather

Terrain

Shelter

Shelter Constructed ☐

Type of Shelter

_____
_____

Clothing/Coverings ☐
Waterproof ☐
Animal proof ☐
Sunproof ☐
Fire Started ☐

Food Inventory

Rations ☐
_____
_____
_____
_____
_____

Water ☐
Hunting ☐
_____
_____
_____

Fishing ☐
_____
_____
_____

Foraging ☐
_____
_____
_____

Journey

Distance Covered

Trail Markers Used

Landmarks Sighted

Animal Prints

Map Sketch

Lat. _____ Long. _____

Party Member	Status	Injuries	Treatment

Date _____

Conditions

Weather

Terrain

Food Inventory

Rations ☐
_____
_____
_____
_____

Water ☐
Hunting ☐
_____
_____
_____

Fishing ☐
_____
_____

Foraging ☐
_____
_____

Journey

Distance Covered

Trail Markers Used

Landmarks Sighted

Animal Prints

Shelter

Shelter Constructed ☐
Type of Shelter
_____
_____

Clothing/Coverings ☐
Waterproof ☐
Animal proof ☐
Sunproof ☐
Fire Started ☐

Map Sketch

Lat. _____ Long. _____

Party Member	Status	Injuries	Treatment

Date _____

Conditions

Weather

Terrain

Shelter

Shelter Constructed ☐

Type of Shelter

_____

_____

_____

Clothing/Coverings ☐

Waterproof ☐

Animal proof ☐

Sunproof ☐

Fire Started ☐

Food Inventory

Rations ☐

_____
_____
_____
_____

Water ☐

Hunting ☐

_____
_____
_____

Fishing ☐

_____
_____
_____

Foraging ☐

_____
_____
_____

Journey

Distance Covered

Trail Markers Used

Landmarks Sighted

Animal Prints

Map Sketch

Lat. _____ Long. _____

Party Member	Status	Injuries	Treatment

Date _____

Conditions

Weather

Terrain

Shelter

Shelter Constructed ☐

Type of Shelter

_____

_____

_____

Clothing/Coverings ☐

Waterproof ☐

Animal proof ☐

Sunproof ☐

Fire Started ☐

Food Inventory

Rations ☐

_____
_____
_____
_____

Water ☐

Hunting ☐

_____
_____
_____

Fishing ☐

_____
_____
_____

Foraging ☐

_____
_____
_____

Journey

Distance Covered

Trail Markers Used

Landmarks Sighted

Animal Prints

Map Sketch

Lat. _____ Long. _____

Party Member	Status	Injuries	Treatment

Date _____

Conditions

Weather

Terrain

Shelter

Shelter Constructed ☐

Type of Shelter

_____

_____

Clothing/Coverings ☐
Waterproof ☐
Animal proof ☐
Sunproof ☐
Fire Started ☐

Food Inventory

Rations ☐

_____
_____
_____
_____

Water ☐
Hunting ☐

_____
_____
_____

Fishing ☐

_____
_____

Foraging ☐

_____
_____

Journey

Distance Covered

Trail Markers Used

Landmarks Sighted

Animal Prints

Map Sketch

Lat. _____ Long. _____

Party Member	Status	Injuries	Treatment

Date _____

Conditions

Weather

Terrain

Shelter

Shelter Constructed ☐

Type of Shelter

_____

_____

_____

Clothing/Coverings ☐

Waterproof ☐

Animal proof ☐

Sunproof ☐

Fire Started ☐

Map Sketch

Lat. _____ Long. _____

Food Inventory

Rations ☐

_____
_____
_____
_____

Water ☐

Hunting ☐

_____
_____
_____

Fishing ☐

_____
_____

Foraging ☐

_____
_____
_____

Journey

Distance Covered

Trail Markers Used

Landmarks Sighted

Animal Prints

Party Member	Status	Injuries	Treatment

Date _____

Conditions

Weather

Terrain

Shelter

Shelter Constructed ☐

Type of Shelter

_____

_____

_____

Clothing/Coverings ☐

Waterproof ☐

Animal proof ☐

Sunproof ☐

Fire Started ☐

Food Inventory

Rations ☐

_____
_____
_____
_____

Water ☐

Hunting ☐

_____
_____
_____

Fishing ☐

_____
_____
_____

Foraging ☐

_____
_____
_____

Journey

Distance Covered

Trail Markers Used

Landmarks Sighted

Animal Prints

Map Sketch

Lat. _____ Long. _____

Party Member	Status	Injuries	Treatment

Date _____

Conditions

Weather

Terrain

Shelter

Shelter Constructed ☐

Type of Shelter

_____

_____

_____

Clothing/Coverings ☐

Waterproof ☐

Animal proof ☐

Sunproof ☐

Fire Started ☐

Food Inventory

Rations ☐

_____
_____
_____
_____

Water ☐

Hunting ☐

_____
_____
_____

Fishing ☐

_____
_____
_____

Foraging ☐

_____
_____
_____

Journey

Distance Covered

Trail Markers Used

Landmarks Sighted

Animal Prints

Map Sketch

Lat. _____ Long. _____

Party Member	Status	Injuries	Treatment

Date _____

Conditions

Weather

Terrain

Shelter

Shelter Constructed ☐

Type of Shelter

_____

_____

Clothing/Coverings ☐
Waterproof ☐
Animal proof ☐
Sunproof ☐
Fire Started ☐

Food Inventory

Rations ☐

_____
_____
_____
_____

Water ☐
Hunting ☐

_____
_____

Fishing ☐

_____
_____

Foraging ☐

_____
_____

Journey

Distance Covered

Trail Markers Used

Landmarks Sighted

Animal Prints

Map Sketch

Lat. _____ Long. _____

Party Member	Status	Injuries	Treatment

Date _____

Conditions

Weather

Terrain

Shelter

Shelter Constructed ☐

Type of Shelter

_____
_____
_____

Clothing/Coverings ☐
Waterproof ☐
Animal proof ☐
Sunproof ☐
Fire Started ☐

Food Inventory

Rations ☐
_____
_____
_____
_____

Water ☐
Hunting ☐
_____
_____
_____

Fishing ☐
_____
_____
_____

Foraging ☐
_____
_____
_____

Journey

Distance Covered

Trail Markers Used

Landmarks Sighted

Animal Prints

Map Sketch

Lat. _____   Long. _____

Party Member	Status	Injuries	Treatment

Date _____

Conditions

Weather

Terrain

Shelter

Shelter Constructed ☐

Type of Shelter

_____

_____

Clothing/Coverings ☐

Waterproof ☐

Animal proof ☐

Sunproof ☐

Fire Started ☐

Food Inventory

Rations ☐

_____
_____
_____
_____

Water ☐

Hunting ☐

_____
_____
_____
_____

Fishing ☐

_____
_____
_____

Foraging ☐

_____
_____
_____

Journey

Distance Covered

Trail Markers Used

Landmarks Sighted

Animal Prints

Map Sketch

Lat. _____ Long. _____

Party Member	Status	Injuries	Treatment

Date _____

Conditions

Weather

Terrain

Shelter

Shelter Constructed ☐

Type of Shelter

_____

_____

_____

Clothing/Coverings ☐

Waterproof ☐

Animal proof ☐

Sunproof ☐

Fire Started ☐

Food Inventory

Rations ☐

_____
_____
_____
_____

Water ☐

Hunting ☐

_____
_____
_____

Fishing ☐

_____
_____
_____

Foraging ☐

_____
_____
_____

Journey

Distance Covered

Trail Markers Used

Landmarks Sighted

Animal Prints

Map Sketch

Lat. _____   Long. _____

Party Member	Status	Injuries	Treatment

Date _____

Conditions

Weather

Terrain

Shelter

Shelter Constructed ☐

Type of Shelter

_____

_____

Clothing/Coverings ☐

Waterproof ☐

Animal proof ☐

Sunproof ☐

Fire Started ☐

Food Inventory

Rations ☐

_____
_____
_____
_____

Water ☐

Hunting ☐

_____
_____
_____

Fishing ☐

_____
_____
_____

Foraging ☐

_____
_____
_____

Journey

Distance Covered

Trail Markers Used

Landmarks Sighted

Animal Prints

Map Sketch

Lat. _____   Long. _____

Party Member	Status	Injuries	Treatment

Date _____

Conditions

Weather

Terrain

Shelter

Shelter Constructed ☐

Type of Shelter

_____

_____

_____

Clothing/Coverings ☐

Waterproof ☐

Animal proof ☐

Sunproof ☐

Fire Started ☐

Food Inventory

Rations ☐

_____
_____
_____
_____

Water ☐

Hunting ☐

_____
_____

Fishing ☐

_____
_____

Foraging ☐

_____
_____

Journey

Distance Covered

Trail Markers Used

Landmarks Sighted

Animal Prints

Map Sketch

Lat. _____   Long. _____

Party Member	Status	Injuries	Treatment

Date _____

Conditions

Weather

Terrain

Shelter

Shelter Constructed ☐

Type of Shelter

_____

_____

Clothing/Coverings ☐
Waterproof ☐
Animal proof ☐
Sunproof ☐
Fire Started ☐

Food Inventory

Rations ☐
_____
_____
_____
_____

Water ☐
Hunting ☐
_____
_____

Fishing ☐
_____
_____

Foraging ☐
_____
_____

Journey

Distance Covered

Trail Markers Used

Landmarks Sighted

Animal Prints

Map Sketch

Lat. _____   Long. _____

Party Member	Status	Injuries	Treatment

Date _____

Conditions

Weather

Terrain

Food Inventory

Rations ☐
_____
_____
_____
_____

Water ☐
Hunting ☐
_____
_____
_____

Fishing ☐
_____
_____
_____

Foraging ☐
_____
_____
_____

Journey

Distance Covered

Trail Markers Used

Landmarks Sighted

Animal Prints

Shelter

Shelter Constructed ☐

Type of Shelter
_____
_____

Clothing/Coverings ☐
Waterproof ☐
Animal proof ☐
Sunproof ☐
Fire Started ☐

Map Sketch

Lat. _____ Long. _____

Party Member	Status	Injuries	Treatment

Date _____

Conditions

Weather

Terrain

Shelter

Shelter Constructed ☐

Type of Shelter

_____

_____

Clothing/Coverings ☐
Waterproof ☐
Animal proof ☐
Sunproof ☐
Fire Started ☐

Food Inventory

Rations ☐
_____
_____
_____
_____

Water ☐
Hunting ☐
_____
_____
_____

Fishing ☐
_____
_____
_____

Foraging ☐
_____
_____
_____

Journey

Distance Covered

Trail Markers Used

Landmarks Sighted

Animal Prints

Map Sketch

Lat. _____   Long. _____

Party Member	Status	Injuries	Treatment

Date _____

Conditions

Weather

Terrain

Shelter

Shelter Constructed ☐

Type of Shelter

_____

_____

_____

Clothing/Coverings ☐
Waterproof ☐
Animal proof ☐
Sunproof ☐
Fire Started ☐

Food Inventory

Rations ☐

_____
_____
_____
_____

Water ☐
Hunting ☐

_____
_____
_____

Fishing ☐

_____
_____
_____

Foraging ☐

_____
_____
_____

Journey

Distance Covered

Trail Markers Used

Landmarks Sighted

Animal Prints

Map Sketch

Lat. _____   Long. _____

Party Member	Status	Injuries	Treatment

Date _____

Conditions

Weather

Terrain

Shelter

Shelter Constructed ☐

Type of Shelter

_____

_____

Clothing/Coverings ☐

Waterproof ☐

Animal proof ☐

Sunproof ☐

Fire Started ☐

Food Inventory

Rations ☐

_____
_____
_____
_____

Water ☐

Hunting ☐

_____
_____
_____

Fishing ☐

_____
_____

Foraging ☐

_____
_____
_____

Journey

Distance Covered

Trail Markers Used

Landmarks Sighted

Animal Prints

Map Sketch

Lat. _____ Long. _____

Party Member	Status	Injuries	Treatment

Date _____

Conditions

Weather

Terrain

Food Inventory

Rations ☐
_____
_____
_____
_____

Water ☐
Hunting ☐
_____
_____
_____

Fishing ☐
_____
_____

Foraging ☐
_____
_____
_____

Journey

Distance Covered

Trail Markers Used

Landmarks Sighted

Animal Prints

Shelter

Shelter Constructed ☐

Type of Shelter
_____
_____
_____

Clothing/Coverings ☐
Waterproof ☐
Animal proof ☐
Sunproof ☐
Fire Started ☐

Map Sketch

Lat. ____ Long. ____

Party Member	Status	Injuries	Treatment

Date _____

Conditions

Weather

Terrain

Shelter

Shelter Constructed ☐

Type of Shelter

_____

_____

Clothing/Coverings ☐
Waterproof ☐
Animal proof ☐
Sunproof ☐
Fire Started ☐

Food Inventory

Rations ☐

_____
_____
_____
_____
_____

Water ☐
Hunting ☐

_____
_____
_____

Fishing ☐

_____
_____

Foraging ☐

_____
_____
_____

Journey

Distance Covered

Trail Markers Used

Landmarks Sighted

Animal Prints

Map Sketch

Lat. _____ Long. _____

Party Member	Status	Injuries	Treatment

Date _____

Conditions

Weather

Terrain

Shelter

Shelter Constructed ☐

Type of Shelter

_____

_____

_____

Clothing/Coverings ☐

Waterproof ☐

Animal proof ☐

Sunproof ☐

Fire Started ☐

Food Inventory

Rations ☐

_____
_____
_____
_____

Water ☐

Hunting ☐

_____
_____
_____

Fishing ☐

_____
_____
_____

Foraging ☐

_____
_____
_____

Journey

Distance Covered

Trail Markers Used

Landmarks Sighted

Animal Prints

Map Sketch

Lat. _____ Long. _____

Party Member	Status	Injuries	Treatment

Date _____

Conditions

Weather

Terrain

Shelter

Shelter Constructed ☐

Type of Shelter

_____

_____

_____

Clothing/Coverings ☐

Waterproof ☐

Animal proof ☐

Sunproof ☐

Fire Started ☐

Food Inventory

Rations ☐
_____
_____
_____
_____

Water ☐

Hunting ☐
_____
_____
_____

Fishing ☐
_____
_____

Foraging ☐
_____
_____
_____

Journey

Distance Covered

Trail Markers Used

Landmarks Sighted

Animal Prints

Map Sketch

Lat. _____ Long. _____

Party Member	Status	Injuries	Treatment

Date _____

Conditions

Weather

Terrain

Shelter

Shelter Constructed ☐

Type of Shelter

_____

_____

Clothing/Coverings ☐

Waterproof ☐

Animal proof ☐

Sunproof ☐

Fire Started ☐

Food Inventory

Rations ☐

_____
_____
_____
_____

Water ☐

Hunting ☐

_____
_____
_____

Fishing ☐

_____
_____
_____

Foraging ☐

_____
_____
_____

Map Sketch

Lat. _____   Long. _____

Journey

Distance Covered

Trail Markers Used

Landmarks Sighted

Animal Prints

Party Member	Status	Injuries	Treatment

Date _____

Conditions

Weather

Terrain

Shelter

Shelter Constructed ☐

Type of Shelter

_____

_____

Clothing/Coverings ☐
Waterproof ☐
Animal proof ☐
Sunproof ☐
Fire Started ☐

Map Sketch

Lat. _____ Long. _____

Food Inventory

Rations ☐
_____
_____
_____
_____

Water ☐
Hunting ☐
_____
_____
_____

Fishing ☐
_____
_____

Foraging ☐
_____
_____

Journey

Distance Covered

Trail Markers Used

Landmarks Sighted

Animal Prints

Party Member	Status	Injuries	Treatment

Date _____

Conditions

Weather

Terrain

Shelter

Shelter Constructed ☐

Type of Shelter

_____
_____

Clothing/Coverings ☐
Waterproof ☐
Animal proof ☐
Sunproof ☐
Fire Started ☐

Food Inventory

Rations ☐
_____
_____
_____
_____

Water ☐
Hunting ☐
_____
_____
_____

Fishing ☐
_____
_____

Foraging ☐
_____
_____
_____

Journey

Distance Covered

Trail Markers Used

Landmarks Sighted

Animal Prints

Map Sketch

Lat. _____ Long. _____

Party Member	Status	Injuries	Treatment

Date _____

Conditions

Weather

Terrain

Shelter

Shelter Constructed ☐

Type of Shelter

_____

_____

_____

Clothing/Coverings ☐

Waterproof ☐

Animal proof ☐

Sunproof ☐

Fire Started ☐

Food Inventory

Rations ☐

_____
_____
_____
_____

Water ☐

Hunting ☐

_____
_____
_____

Fishing ☐

_____
_____

Foraging ☐

_____
_____
_____

Journey

Distance Covered

Trail Markers Used

Landmarks Sighted

Animal Prints

Map Sketch

Lat. _____ Long. _____

Party Member	Status	Injuries	Treatment

Date _____

Conditions

Weather

Terrain

Shelter

Shelter Constructed ☐

Type of Shelter

_____

_____

_____

Clothing/Coverings ☐

Waterproof ☐

Animal proof ☐

Sunproof ☐

Fire Started ☐

Map Sketch

Lat. _____ Long. _____

Food Inventory

Rations ☐

_____
_____
_____
_____

Water ☐

Hunting ☐

_____
_____
_____

Fishing ☐

_____
_____
_____

Foraging ☐

_____
_____
_____

Journey

Distance Covered

Trail Markers Used

Landmarks Sighted

Animal Prints

Party Member	Status	Injuries	Treatment

Date _____

Conditions

Weather

Terrain

Shelter

Shelter Constructed ☐

Type of Shelter

_____

_____

Clothing/Coverings ☐
Waterproof ☐
Animal proof ☐
Sunproof ☐
Fire Started ☐

Food Inventory

Rations ☐
_____
_____
_____
_____

Water ☐
Hunting ☐
_____
_____
_____

Fishing ☐
_____
_____

Foraging ☐
_____
_____
_____

Map Sketch

Lat. _____   Long. _____

Journey

Distance Covered

Trail Markers Used

Landmarks Sighted

Animal Prints

Party Member	Status	Injuries	Treatment

Date _____

Conditions

Weather

Terrain

Shelter

Shelter Constructed ☐

Type of Shelter

_____

_____

Clothing/Coverings ☐

Waterproof ☐

Animal proof ☐

Sunproof ☐

Fire Started ☐

Map Sketch

Lat. _____   Long. _____

Food Inventory

Rations ☐

_____
_____
_____
_____

Water ☐

Hunting ☐

_____
_____
_____

Fishing ☐

_____
_____
_____

Foraging ☐

_____
_____
_____

Journey

Distance Covered

Trail Markers Used

Landmarks Sighted

Animal Prints

Party Member	Status	Injuries	Treatment

Date _____

Conditions

Weather

Terrain

Shelter

Shelter Constructed ☐

Type of Shelter

_____

_____

Clothing/Coverings ☐
Waterproof ☐
Animal proof ☐
Sunproof ☐
Fire Started ☐

Food Inventory

Rations ☐
_____
_____
_____
_____

Water ☐
Hunting ☐
_____
_____
_____

Fishing ☐
_____
_____

Foraging ☐
_____
_____
_____

Journey

Distance Covered

Trail Markers Used

Landmarks Sighted

Animal Prints

Map Sketch

Lat. _____ Long. _____

Party Member	Status	Injuries	Treatment

Date _____

Conditions

Weather

Terrain

Shelter

Shelter Constructed ☐

Type of Shelter

_____

_____

Clothing/Coverings ☐

Waterproof ☐

Animal proof ☐

Sunproof ☐

Fire Started ☐

Food Inventory

Rations ☐

_____
_____
_____
_____

Water ☐

Hunting ☐

_____
_____
_____

Fishing ☐

_____
_____
_____

Foraging ☐

_____
_____
_____

Journey

Distance Covered

Trail Markers Used

Landmarks Sighted

Animal Prints

Map Sketch

Lat.   Long.

Party Member	Status	Injuries	Treatment

Date _____

Conditions

Weather

Terrain

Shelter

Shelter Constructed ☐

Type of Shelter

_____

_____

Clothing/Coverings ☐
Waterproof ☐
Animal proof ☐
Sunproof ☐
Fire Started ☐

Food Inventory

Rations ☐

_____
_____
_____
_____

Water ☐
Hunting ☐

_____
_____

Fishing ☐

_____
_____

Foraging ☐

_____
_____

Journey

Distance Covered

Trail Markers Used

Landmarks Sighted

Animal Prints

Map Sketch

Lat. Long.

Party Member	Status	Injuries	Treatment

Date _____

Conditions

Weather

Terrain

Shelter

Shelter Constructed ☐

Type of Shelter

_____
_____
_____

Clothing/Coverings ☐
Waterproof ☐
Animal proof ☐
Sunproof ☐
Fire Started ☐

Food Inventory

Rations ☐
_____
_____
_____
_____

Water ☐
Hunting ☐
_____
_____
_____

Fishing ☐
_____
_____
_____

Foraging ☐
_____
_____
_____

Journey

Distance Covered

Trail Markers Used

Landmarks Sighted

Animal Prints

Map Sketch

Lat. _____ Long. _____

Party Member	Status	Injuries	Treatment

Date _____

Conditions

Weather

Terrain

Shelter

Shelter Constructed ☐

Type of Shelter

_____

_____

_____

Clothing/Coverings ☐

Waterproof ☐

Animal proof ☐

Sunproof ☐

Fire Started ☐

Map Sketch

Lat. _____ Long. _____

Food Inventory

Rations ☐

_____
_____
_____
_____

Water ☐

Hunting ☐

_____
_____
_____

Fishing ☐

_____
_____
_____

Foraging ☐

_____
_____
_____

Journey

Distance Covered

Trail Markers Used

Landmarks Sighted

Animal Prints

Party Member	Status	Injuries	Treatment

Date _____

Conditions

Weather

Terrain

Shelter

Shelter Constructed ☐

Type of Shelter

_____

_____

_____

Clothing/Coverings ☐

Waterproof ☐

Animal proof ☐

Sunproof ☐

Fire Started ☐

Map Sketch

Lat. _____   Long. _____

Food Inventory

Rations ☐

_____
_____
_____
_____

Water ☐

Hunting ☐

_____
_____
_____

Fishing ☐

_____
_____
_____

Foraging ☐

_____
_____
_____

Journey

Distance Covered

Trail Markers Used

Landmarks Sighted

Animal Prints

Party Member	Status	Injuries	Treatment

Date _____

Conditions

Weather

Terrain

Shelter

Shelter Constructed ☐

Type of Shelter

_____

_____

_____

Clothing/Coverings ☐
Waterproof ☐
Animal proof ☐
Sunproof ☐
Fire Started ☐

Map Sketch

Lat. _____ Long. _____

Food Inventory

Rations ☐
_____
_____
_____
_____

Water ☐
Hunting ☐
_____
_____
_____

Fishing ☐
_____
_____
_____

Foraging ☐
_____
_____
_____

Journey

Distance Covered

Trail Markers Used

Landmarks Sighted

Animal Prints

Party Member	Status	Injuries	Treatment

Date _____

Conditions

Weather

Terrain

Shelter

Shelter Constructed ☐

Type of Shelter

_____

_____

Clothing/Coverings ☐

Waterproof ☐

Animal proof ☐

Sunproof ☐

Fire Started ☐

Map Sketch

Lat. _____ Long. _____

Food Inventory

Rations ☐

_____
_____
_____
_____

Water ☐

Hunting ☐

_____
_____
_____

Fishing ☐

_____
_____
_____

Foraging ☐

_____
_____
_____

Journey

Distance Covered

Trail Markers Used

Landmarks Sighted

Animal Prints

Party Member	Status	Injuries	Treatment

Date _____

Conditions

Weather

Terrain

Food Inventory

Rations ☐

_____
_____
_____
_____

Water ☐

Hunting ☐

_____
_____
_____

Fishing ☐

_____
_____

Foraging ☐

_____
_____

Journey

Distance Covered

Trail Markers Used

Landmarks Sighted

Animal Prints

Shelter

Shelter Constructed ☐

Type of Shelter

_____
_____

Clothing/Coverings ☐
Waterproof ☐
Animal proof ☐
Sunproof ☐
Fire Started ☐

Map Sketch

Lat. _____   Long. _____

Party Member	Status	Injuries	Treatment

Date _____

Conditions

Weather

Terrain

Shelter

Shelter Constructed ☐

Type of Shelter

_____

_____

Clothing/Coverings ☐
Waterproof ☐
Animal proof ☐
Sunproof ☐
Fire Started ☐

Food Inventory

Rations ☐
_____
_____
_____
_____

Water ☐
Hunting ☐
_____
_____
_____

Fishing ☐
_____
_____
_____

Foraging ☐
_____
_____
_____

Journey

Distance Covered

Trail Markers Used

Landmarks Sighted

Animal Prints

Map Sketch

Lat. _____ Long. _____

Party Member	Status	Injuries	Treatment

Date _____

Conditions

Weather

Terrain

Shelter

Shelter Constructed ☐

Type of Shelter

_____

_____

Clothing/Coverings ☐
Waterproof ☐
Animal proof ☐
Sunproof ☐
Fire Started ☐

Food Inventory

Rations ☐

_____
_____
_____
_____

Water ☐
Hunting ☐

_____
_____
_____

Fishing ☐

_____
_____
_____

Foraging ☐

_____
_____
_____

Journey

Distance Covered

Trail Markers Used

Landmarks Sighted

Animal Prints

Map Sketch

Lat. _____   Long. _____

Party Member	Status	Injuries	Treatment

Date _____

Conditions

Weather

Terrain

Shelter

Shelter Constructed ☐

Type of Shelter

_____

_____

Clothing/Coverings ☐

Waterproof ☐

Animal proof ☐

Sunproof ☐

Fire Started ☐

Map Sketch

Lat. ___   Long. ___

Food Inventory

Rations ☐

_____
_____
_____
_____

Water ☐

Hunting ☐

_____
_____
_____

Fishing ☐

_____
_____
_____

Foraging ☐

_____
_____
_____

Journey

Distance Covered

Trail Markers Used

Landmarks Sighted

Animal Prints

Party Member	Status	Injuries	Treatment

Date _____

Conditions

Weather

Terrain

Shelter

Shelter Constructed ☐

Type of Shelter

_____

_____

Clothing/Coverings ☐
Waterproof ☐
Animal proof ☐
Sunproof ☐
Fire Started ☐

Food Inventory

Rations ☐
_____
_____
_____
_____

Water ☐
Hunting ☐
_____
_____
_____

Fishing ☐
_____
_____
_____

Foraging ☐
_____
_____
_____

Journey

Distance Covered

Trail Markers Used

Landmarks Sighted

Animal Prints

Map Sketch

Lat. _____ Long. _____

Party Member	Status	Injuries	Treatment

Date _____

Conditions

Weather

Terrain

Food Inventory

Rations ☐

_____
_____
_____
_____

Water ☐

Hunting ☐

_____
_____
_____

Fishing ☐

_____
_____
_____

Foraging ☐

_____
_____
_____

Journey

Distance Covered

Trail Markers Used

Landmarks Sighted

Animal Prints

Shelter

Shelter Constructed ☐

Type of Shelter

_____
_____
_____

Clothing/Coverings ☐

Waterproof ☐

Animal proof ☐

Sunproof ☐

Fire Started ☐

Map Sketch

Lat. ____   Long. ____

Party Member	Status	Injuries	Treatment

Date _____

Conditions

Weather

Terrain

Shelter

Shelter Constructed ☐

Type of Shelter

_____
_____

Clothing/Coverings ☐
Waterproof ☐
Animal proof ☐
Sunproof ☐
Fire Started ☐

Map Sketch

Lat. _____ Long. _____

Food Inventory

Rations ☐
_____
_____
_____
_____

Water ☐
Hunting ☐
_____
_____
_____

Fishing ☐
_____
_____
_____

Foraging ☐
_____
_____
_____

Journey

Distance Covered

Trail Markers Used

Landmarks Sighted

Animal Prints

Party Member	Status	Injuries	Treatment

Date _____

Conditions

Weather

Terrain

Shelter

Shelter Constructed ☐

Type of Shelter

_____

_____

Clothing/Coverings ☐

Waterproof ☐

Animal proof ☐

Sunproof ☐

Fire Started ☐

Map Sketch

Lat. _____ Long. _____

Food Inventory

Rations ☐

_____
_____
_____
_____

Water ☐

Hunting ☐

_____
_____
_____

Fishing ☐

_____
_____
_____

Foraging ☐

_____
_____
_____

Journey

Distance Covered

Trail Markers Used

Landmarks Sighted

Animal Prints

Party Member	Status	Injuries	Treatment

Date _____

Conditions

Weather

Terrain

Shelter

Shelter Constructed ☐

Type of Shelter

_____

_____

Clothing/Coverings ☐
Waterproof ☐
Animal proof ☐
Sunproof ☐
Fire Started ☐

Map Sketch

Lat. _____ Long. _____

Food Inventory

Rations ☐
_____
_____
_____
_____
_____

Water ☐
Hunting ☐
_____
_____
_____

Fishing ☐
_____
_____
_____

Foraging ☐
_____
_____

Journey

Distance Covered

Trail Markers Used

Landmarks Sighted

Animal Prints

Party Member	Status	Injuries	Treatment

Date _____

Conditions

Weather

Terrain

Food Inventory

Rations ☐
_____
_____
_____
_____

Water ☐
Hunting ☐
_____
_____
_____

Fishing ☐
_____
_____

Foraging ☐
_____
_____
_____

Journey

Distance Covered

Trail Markers Used

Landmarks Sighted

Animal Prints

Shelter

Shelter Constructed ☐
Type of Shelter
_____
_____

Clothing/Coverings ☐
Waterproof ☐
Animal proof ☐
Sunproof ☐
Fire Started ☐

Map Sketch

Lat. _____   Long. _____

Party Member	Status	Injuries	Treatment

Date _____

Conditions

Weather

Terrain

Shelter

Shelter Constructed ☐

Type of Shelter

_____

_____

Clothing/Coverings ☐

Waterproof ☐

Animal proof ☐

Sunproof ☐

Fire Started ☐

Map Sketch

Lat. _____ Long. _____

Food Inventory

Rations ☐

_____
_____
_____
_____

Water ☐

Hunting ☐

_____
_____
_____

Fishing ☐

_____
_____

Foraging ☐

_____
_____
_____

Journey

Distance Covered

Trail Markers Used

Landmarks Sighted

Animal Prints

Party Member	Status	Injuries	Treatment

Date _____

Conditions

Weather

Terrain

Shelter

Shelter Constructed ☐

Type of Shelter
_____
_____

Clothing/Coverings ☐
Waterproof ☐
Animal proof ☐
Sunproof ☐
Fire Started ☐

Food Inventory

Rations ☐
_____
_____
_____
_____

Water ☐
Hunting ☐
_____
_____
_____

Fishing ☐
_____
_____
_____

Foraging ☐
_____
_____
_____

Journey

Distance Covered

Trail Markers Used

Landmarks Sighted

Animal Prints

Map Sketch

Lat. _____ Long. _____

Party Member	Status	Injuries	Treatment

Date _____

Conditions

Weather

Terrain

Shelter

Shelter Constructed ☐

Type of Shelter

_____

_____

Clothing/Coverings ☐
Waterproof ☐
Animal proof ☐
Sunproof ☐
Fire Started ☐

Food Inventory

Rations ☐
_____
_____
_____
_____

Water ☐
Hunting ☐
_____
_____

Fishing ☐
_____
_____

Foraging ☐
_____
_____

Journey

Distance Covered

Trail Markers Used

Landmarks Sighted

Animal Prints

Map Sketch

Lat. _____ Long. _____

Party Member	Status	Injuries	Treatment

Date _____

Conditions

Weather

Terrain

Shelter

Shelter Constructed ☐

Type of Shelter

_____
_____
_____

Clothing/Coverings ☐
Waterproof ☐
Animal proof ☐
Sunproof ☐
Fire Started ☐

Food Inventory

Rations ☐
_____
_____
_____
_____
_____

Water ☐
Hunting ☐
_____
_____
_____

Fishing ☐
_____
_____
_____

Foraging ☐
_____
_____
_____

Map Sketch

Lat. _____ Long. _____

Journey

Distance Covered

Trail Markers Used

Landmarks Sighted

Animal Prints

Party Member	Status	Injuries	Treatment

Date _____

Conditions

Weather

Terrain

Shelter

Shelter Constructed ☐

Type of Shelter

_____
_____
_____

Clothing/Coverings ☐
Waterproof ☐
Animal proof ☐
Sunproof ☐
Fire Started ☐

Map Sketch

Lat. _____   Long. _____

Food Inventory

Rations ☐
_____
_____
_____
_____

Water ☐
Hunting ☐
_____
_____
_____

Fishing ☐
_____
_____
_____

Foraging ☐
_____
_____
_____

Journey

Distance Covered

Trail Markers Used

Landmarks Sighted

Animal Prints

Party Member	Status	Injuries	Treatment

Date _____

Conditions

Weather

Terrain

Shelter

Shelter Constructed ☐

Type of Shelter

_____

_____

Clothing/Coverings ☐

Waterproof ☐

Animal proof ☐

Sunproof ☐

Fire Started ☐

Food Inventory

Rations ☐

_____
_____
_____
_____

Water ☐

Hunting ☐

_____
_____
_____

Fishing ☐

_____
_____
_____

Foraging ☐

_____
_____
_____

Journey

Distance Covered

Trail Markers Used

Landmarks Sighted

Animal Prints

Map Sketch

Lat. _____   Long. _____

Party Member	Status	Injuries	Treatment

Date _____

Conditions

Weather

Terrain

Shelter

Shelter Constructed ☐

Type of Shelter

_____

_____

Clothing/Coverings ☐
Waterproof ☐
Animal proof ☐
Sunproof ☐
Fire Started ☐

Food Inventory

Rations ☐
_____
_____
_____
_____

Water ☐
Hunting ☐
_____
_____
_____

Fishing ☐
_____
_____

Foraging ☐
_____
_____

Journey

Distance Covered

Trail Markers Used

Landmarks Sighted

Animal Prints

Map Sketch

Lat. _____ Long. _____

Party Member	Status	Injuries	Treatment

Date _____

Conditions

Weather

Terrain

Shelter

Shelter Constructed ☐

Type of Shelter

_____

_____

Clothing/Coverings ☐

Waterproof ☐

Animal proof ☐

Sunproof ☐

Fire Started ☐

Map Sketch

Lat. _____ Long. _____

Food Inventory

Rations ☐

_____
_____
_____
_____

Water ☐

Hunting ☐

_____
_____
_____

Fishing ☐

_____
_____
_____

Foraging ☐

_____
_____
_____

Journey

Distance Covered

Trail Markers Used

Landmarks Sighted

Animal Prints

Party Member	Status	Injuries	Treatment

Date _____

Conditions

Weather

Terrain

Shelter

Shelter Constructed ☐

Type of Shelter

_____

_____

Clothing/Coverings ☐

Waterproof ☐

Animal proof ☐

Sunproof ☐

Fire Started ☐

Food Inventory

Rations ☐

_____
_____
_____
_____

Water ☐

Hunting ☐

_____
_____
_____

Fishing ☐

_____
_____

Foraging ☐

_____
_____
_____

Journey

Distance Covered

Trail Markers Used

Landmarks Sighted

Animal Prints

Map Sketch

Lat. _____ Long. _____

Party Member	Status	Injuries	Treatment

Date _____

Conditions

Weather

Terrain

Shelter

Shelter Constructed ☐

Type of Shelter

_____

_____

Clothing/Coverings ☐

Waterproof ☐

Animal proof ☐

Sunproof ☐

Fire Started ☐

Food Inventory

Rations ☐

_____
_____
_____
_____

Water ☐

Hunting ☐

_____
_____
_____

Fishing ☐

_____
_____
_____

Foraging ☐

_____
_____
_____

Journey

Distance Covered

Trail Markers Used

Landmarks Sighted

Animal Prints

Map Sketch

Lat. _____ Long. _____

Party Member	Status	Injuries	Treatment

Date _____

Conditions

Weather

Terrain

Shelter

Shelter Constructed ☐

Type of Shelter

_____

_____

Clothing/Coverings ☐

Waterproof ☐

Animal proof ☐

Sunproof ☐

Fire Started ☐

Map Sketch

Lat. _____ Long. _____

Food Inventory

Rations ☐

_____
_____
_____
_____

Water ☐

Hunting ☐

_____
_____
_____

Fishing ☐

_____
_____
_____

Foraging ☐

_____
_____
_____

Journey

Distance Covered

Trail Markers Used

Landmarks Sighted

Animal Prints

Party Member	Status	Injuries	Treatment

Date _____

Conditions

Weather

Terrain

Shelter

Shelter Constructed ☐

Type of Shelter

_____

_____

_____

Clothing/Coverings ☐
Waterproof ☐
Animal proof ☐
Sunproof ☐
Fire Started ☐

Food Inventory

Rations ☐

_____
_____
_____
_____

Water ☐
Hunting ☐

_____
_____
_____

Fishing ☐

_____
_____
_____

Foraging ☐

_____
_____
_____

Journey

Distance Covered

Trail Markers Used

Landmarks Sighted

Animal Prints

Map Sketch

Lat. _____ Long. _____

Party Member	Status	Injuries	Treatment

Date _____

Conditions

Weather

Terrain

Shelter

Shelter Constructed ☐

Type of Shelter

_____

_____

Clothing/Coverings ☐
Waterproof ☐
Animal proof ☐
Sunproof ☐
Fire Started ☐

Food Inventory

Rations ☐

_____
_____
_____
_____

Water ☐
Hunting ☐

_____
_____
_____

Fishing ☐

_____
_____

Foraging ☐

_____
_____
_____

Map Sketch

Lat. _____ Long. _____

Journey

Distance Covered

Trail Markers Used

Landmarks Sighted

Animal Prints

Party Member	Status	Injuries	Treatment

Date _____

Conditions

Weather

Terrain

Shelter

Shelter Constructed ☐
Type of Shelter

_____

_____

Clothing/Coverings ☐
Waterproof ☐
Animal proof ☐
Sunproof ☐
Fire Started ☐

Food Inventory

Rations ☐

_____
_____
_____
_____

Water ☐
Hunting ☐

_____
_____

Fishing ☐

_____
_____

Foraging ☐

_____
_____
_____

Journey

Distance Covered

Trail Markers Used

Landmarks Sighted

Animal Prints

Map Sketch

Lat.　　　Long.

Party Member	Status	Injuries	Treatment

Date _____

Conditions

Weather

Terrain

Shelter

Shelter Constructed ☐
Type of Shelter

_____
_____

Clothing/Coverings ☐
Waterproof ☐
Animal proof ☐
Sunproof ☐
Fire Started ☐

Food Inventory

Rations ☐
_____
_____
_____
_____

Water ☐
Hunting ☐
_____
_____
_____
_____

Fishing ☐
_____
_____

Foraging ☐
_____
_____
_____

Journey

Distance Covered

Trail Markers Used

Landmarks Sighted

Animal Prints

Map Sketch

Lat. _____ Long. _____

Party Member	Status	Injuries	Treatment

Date _____

Conditions

Weather

Terrain

Shelter

Shelter Constructed ☐

Type of Shelter

_____
_____
_____

Clothing/Coverings ☐
Waterproof ☐
Animal proof ☐
Sunproof ☐
Fire Started ☐

Food Inventory

Rations ☐
_____
_____
_____
_____

Water ☐
Hunting ☐
_____
_____
_____

Fishing ☐
_____
_____

Foraging ☐
_____
_____
_____

Journey

Distance Covered

Trail Markers Used

Landmarks Sighted

Animal Prints

Map Sketch

Lat. _____ Long. _____

Party Member	Status	Injuries	Treatment

Date _____

Conditions

Weather

Terrain

Shelter

Shelter Constructed ☐

Type of Shelter

_____
_____
_____

Clothing/Coverings ☐
Waterproof ☐
Animal proof ☐
Sunproof ☐
Fire Started ☐

Food Inventory

Rations ☐
_____
_____
_____
_____

Water ☐
Hunting ☐
_____
_____
_____

Fishing ☐
_____
_____
_____

Foraging ☐
_____
_____
_____

Journey

Distance Covered

Trail Markers Used

Landmarks Sighted

Animal Prints

Map Sketch

Lat. _____ Long. _____

Party Member	Status	Injuries	Treatment

Date _____

Conditions

Weather

Terrain

Shelter

Shelter Constructed ☐

Type of Shelter

_____

_____

Clothing/Coverings ☐
Waterproof ☐
Animal proof ☐
Sunproof ☐
Fire Started ☐

Food Inventory

Rations ☐

_____
_____
_____
_____

Water ☐
Hunting ☐

_____
_____
_____

Fishing ☐

_____
_____

Foraging ☐

_____
_____
_____

Journey

Distance Covered

Trail Markers Used

Landmarks Sighted

Animal Prints

Map Sketch

Lat. _____ Long. _____

Party Member	Status	Injuries	Treatment

Date _____

Conditions

Weather

Terrain

Shelter

Shelter Constructed ☐

Type of Shelter

_____

_____

Clothing/Coverings ☐
Waterproof ☐
Animal proof ☐
Sunproof ☐
Fire Started ☐

Food Inventory

Rations ☐

_____
_____
_____
_____

Water ☐
Hunting ☐

_____
_____
_____

Fishing ☐

_____
_____

Foraging ☐

_____
_____
_____

Journey

Distance Covered

Trail Markers Used

Landmarks Sighted

Animal Prints

Map Sketch

Lat. _____ Long. _____

Party Member	Status	Injuries	Treatment

Date _____

Conditions

Weather

Terrain

Shelter

Shelter Constructed ☐

Type of Shelter

_____
_____

Clothing/Coverings ☐
Waterproof ☐
Animal proof ☐
Sunproof ☐
Fire Started ☐

Food Inventory

Rations ☐
_____
_____
_____
_____

Water ☐
Hunting ☐
_____
_____
_____

Fishing ☐
_____
_____
_____

Foraging ☐
_____
_____
_____

Journey

Distance Covered

Trail Markers Used

Landmarks Sighted

Animal Prints

Map Sketch

Lat. _____   Long. _____

Party Member	Status	Injuries	Treatment

Date _____

Conditions

Weather

Terrain

Shelter

Shelter Constructed ☐

Type of Shelter

_____

_____

Clothing/Coverings ☐

Waterproof ☐

Animal proof ☐

Sunproof ☐

Fire Started ☐

Food Inventory

Rations ☐

_____
_____
_____
_____

Water ☐

Hunting ☐

_____
_____
_____

Fishing ☐

_____
_____
_____

Foraging ☐

_____
_____

Journey

Distance Covered

Trail Markers Used

Landmarks Sighted

Animal Prints

Map Sketch

Lat. _____ Long. _____

Party Member	Status	Injuries	Treatment

Date _____

Conditions

Weather

Terrain

Shelter

Shelter Constructed ☐

Type of Shelter

_____

_____

Clothing/Coverings ☐

Waterproof ☐

Animal proof ☐

Sunproof ☐

Fire Started ☐

Map Sketch

Lat. _____ Long. _____

Food Inventory

Rations ☐

_____
_____
_____
_____

Water ☐

Hunting ☐

_____
_____
_____

Fishing ☐

_____
_____
_____

Foraging ☐

_____
_____
_____

Journey

Distance Covered

Trail Markers Used

Landmarks Sighted

Animal Prints

Party Member	Status	Injuries	Treatment

Date _____

Conditions

Weather

Terrain

Food Inventory

Rations ☐

_____
_____
_____

Water ☐
Hunting ☐

_____
_____

Fishing ☐

_____
_____

Foraging ☐

_____
_____

Journey

Distance Covered

Trail Markers Used

Landmarks Sighted

Animal Prints

Shelter

Shelter Constructed ☐

Type of Shelter

_____
_____
_____

Clothing/Coverings ☐
Waterproof ☐
Animal proof ☐
Sunproof ☐
Fire Started ☐

Map Sketch

Lat. _____   Long. _____

Party Member	Status	Injuries	Treatment

Date _____

Conditions

Weather

Terrain

Shelter

Shelter Constructed ☐

Type of Shelter

_____

_____

Clothing/Coverings ☐

Waterproof ☐

Animal proof ☐

Sunproof ☐

Fire Started ☐

Food Inventory

Rations ☐

_____
_____
_____
_____

Water ☐

Hunting ☐

_____
_____
_____

Fishing ☐

_____
_____
_____

Foraging ☐

_____
_____
_____

Journey

Distance Covered

Trail Markers Used

Landmarks Sighted

Animal Prints

Map Sketch

Lat. _____   Long. _____

Party Member	Status	Injuries	Treatment

Date _____

Conditions

Weather

Terrain

Shelter

Shelter Constructed ☐

Type of Shelter

_____
_____

Clothing/Coverings ☐
Waterproof ☐
Animal proof ☐
Sunproof ☐
Fire Started ☐

Food Inventory

Rations ☐
_____
_____
_____
_____

Water ☐
Hunting ☐
_____
_____
_____

Fishing ☐
_____
_____
_____

Foraging ☐
_____
_____
_____

Map Sketch

Lat. _____ Long. _____

Journey

Distance Covered

Trail Markers Used

Landmarks Sighted

Animal Prints

Party Member	Status	Injuries	Treatment

Date _____

Conditions

Weather

Terrain

Shelter

Shelter Constructed ☐

Type of Shelter

_____
_____

Clothing/Coverings ☐
Waterproof ☐
Animal proof ☐
Sunproof ☐
Fire Started ☐

Food Inventory

Rations ☐
_____
_____
_____
_____

Water ☐
Hunting ☐
_____
_____
_____

Fishing ☐
_____
_____
_____

Foraging ☐
_____
_____

Map Sketch

Lat.   Long.

Journey

Distance Covered

Trail Markers Used

Landmarks Sighted

Animal Prints

Party Member	Status	Injuries	Treatment

Date _____

Conditions

Weather

Terrain

Shelter

Shelter Constructed ☐

Type of Shelter

_____

_____

Clothing/Coverings ☐
Waterproof ☐
Animal proof ☐
Sunproof ☐
Fire Started ☐

Map Sketch

Lat. _____   Long. _____

Food Inventory

Rations ☐
_____
_____
_____
_____

Water ☐
Hunting ☐
_____
_____
_____

Fishing ☐
_____
_____

Foraging ☐
_____
_____

Journey

Distance Covered

Trail Markers Used

Landmarks Sighted

Animal Prints

Party Member	Status	Injuries	Treatment

Date _____

Conditions

Weather

Terrain

Shelter

Shelter Constructed ☐

Type of Shelter

_____

_____

_____

Clothing/Coverings ☐

Waterproof ☐

Animal proof ☐

Sunproof ☐

Fire Started ☐

Food Inventory

Rations ☐

_____
_____
_____
_____

Water ☐

Hunting ☐

_____
_____
_____

Fishing ☐

_____
_____

Foraging ☐

_____
_____
_____

Journey

Distance Covered

Trail Markers Used

Landmarks Sighted

Animal Prints

Map Sketch

Lat. _____   Long. _____

Party Member	Status	Injuries	Treatment

Date _____

Conditions

Weather

Terrain

Shelter

Shelter Constructed ☐

Type of Shelter

_____
_____
_____

Clothing/Coverings ☐
Waterproof ☐
Animal proof ☐
Sunproof ☐
Fire Started ☐

Food Inventory

Rations ☐
_____
_____
_____
_____

Water ☐
Hunting ☐
_____
_____
_____

Fishing ☐
_____
_____

Foraging ☐
_____
_____

Journey

Distance Covered

Trail Markers Used

Landmarks Sighted

Animal Prints

Map Sketch

Lat. _____ Long. _____

Party Member	Status	Injuries	Treatment

Date _____

Conditions

Weather

Terrain

Shelter

Shelter Constructed ☐

Type of Shelter

_____
_____
_____

Clothing/Coverings ☐
Waterproof ☐
Animal proof ☐
Sunproof ☐
Fire Started ☐

Food Inventory

Rations ☐
_____
_____
_____
_____

Water ☐
Hunting ☐
_____
_____
_____

Fishing ☐
_____
_____

Foraging ☐
_____
_____

Map Sketch

Lat. _____ Long. _____

Journey

Distance Covered

Trail Markers Used

Landmarks Sighted

Animal Prints

Party Member	Status	Injuries	Treatment

Date _____

Conditions

Weather

Terrain

Shelter

Shelter Constructed ☐

Type of Shelter

_____

_____

_____

Clothing/Coverings ☐

Waterproof ☐

Animal proof ☐

Sunproof ☐

Fire Started ☐

Map Sketch

Lat. _____ Long. _____

Food Inventory

Rations ☐

_____
_____
_____
_____

Water ☐

Hunting ☐

_____
_____
_____

Fishing ☐

_____
_____
_____

Foraging ☐

_____
_____
_____

Journey

Distance Covered

Trail Markers Used

Landmarks Sighted

Animal Prints

Party Member	Status	Injuries	Treatment

Date _____

Conditions

Weather

Terrain

Shelter

Shelter Constructed ☐

Type of Shelter

_____

_____

_____

Clothing/Coverings ☐

Waterproof ☐

Animal proof ☐

Sunproof ☐

Fire Started ☐

Map Sketch

Lat. _____ Long. _____

Food Inventory

Rations ☐

_____
_____
_____
_____

Water ☐

Hunting ☐

_____
_____
_____

Fishing ☐

_____
_____
_____

Foraging ☐

_____
_____
_____

Journey

Distance Covered

Trail Markers Used

Landmarks Sighted

Animal Prints

Party Member	Status	Injuries	Treatment

Date _____

Conditions

Weather

Terrain

Shelter

Shelter Constructed ☐

Type of Shelter

_____

_____

Clothing/Coverings ☐
Waterproof ☐
Animal proof ☐
Sunproof ☐
Fire Started ☐

Food Inventory

Rations ☐
_____
_____
_____
_____

Water ☐
Hunting ☐
_____
_____
_____

Fishing ☐
_____
_____
_____

Foraging ☐
_____
_____
_____

Journey

Distance Covered

Trail Markers Used

Landmarks Sighted

Animal Prints

Map Sketch

Lat. _____ Long. _____

Party Member	Status	Injuries	Treatment

Date _____

Conditions

Weather

Terrain

Shelter

Shelter Constructed ☐

Type of Shelter

_____

_____

Clothing/Coverings ☐
Waterproof ☐
Animal proof ☐
Sunproof ☐
Fire Started ☐

Food Inventory

Rations ☐

_____
_____
_____
_____

Water ☐
Hunting ☐

_____
_____
_____

Fishing ☐

_____
_____

Foraging ☐

_____
_____
_____

Journey

Distance Covered

Trail Markers Used

Landmarks Sighted

Animal Prints

Map Sketch

Lat. _____ Long. _____

Party Member	Status	Injuries	Treatment

Date _____

Conditions

Weather

Terrain

Shelter

Shelter Constructed ☐

Type of Shelter

_____

_____

_____

Clothing/Coverings ☐
Waterproof ☐
Animal proof ☐
Sunproof ☐
Fire Started ☐

Map Sketch

Lat. _____   Long. _____

Food Inventory

Rations ☐

_____
_____
_____
_____

Water ☐
Hunting ☐

_____
_____
_____

Fishing ☐

_____
_____
_____

Foraging ☐

_____
_____
_____

Journey

Distance Covered

Trail Markers Used

Landmarks Sighted

Animal Prints

Party Member	Status	Injuries	Treatment

Date _____

Conditions

Weather

Terrain

Shelter

Shelter Constructed ☐

Type of Shelter

_____

_____

Clothing/Coverings ☐
Waterproof ☐
Animal proof ☐
Sunproof ☐
Fire Started ☐

Map Sketch

Lat. _____ Long. _____

Food Inventory

Rations ☐
_____
_____
_____
_____

Water ☐
Hunting ☐
_____
_____
_____

Fishing ☐
_____
_____
_____

Foraging ☐
_____
_____
_____

Journey

Distance Covered

Trail Markers Used

Landmarks Sighted

Animal Prints

Party Member	Status	Injuries	Treatment

Date _____

Conditions

Weather

Terrain

Shelter

Shelter Constructed ☐

Type of Shelter

_____
_____

Clothing/Coverings ☐
Waterproof ☐
Animal proof ☐
Sunproof ☐
Fire Started ☐

Food Inventory

Rations ☐
_____
_____
_____
_____

Water ☐
Hunting ☐
_____
_____
_____

Fishing ☐
_____
_____
_____

Foraging ☐
_____
_____
_____

Journey

Distance Covered

Trail Markers Used

Landmarks Sighted

Animal Prints

Map Sketch

Lat. _____ Long. _____

Party Member	Status	Injuries	Treatment

Date _____

Conditions

Weather

Terrain

Shelter

Shelter Constructed ☐

Type of Shelter

_____

_____

_____

Clothing/Coverings ☐
Waterproof ☐
Animal proof ☐
Sunproof ☐
Fire Started ☐

Food Inventory

Rations ☐

_____
_____
_____
_____

Water ☐
Hunting ☐

_____
_____
_____

Fishing ☐

_____
_____
_____

Foraging ☐

_____
_____
_____

Journey

Distance Covered

Trail Markers Used

Landmarks Sighted

Animal Prints

Map Sketch

Lat. _____ Long. _____

Party Member	Status	Injuries	Treatment

Date _____

Conditions

Weather

Terrain

Shelter

Shelter Constructed ☐

Type of Shelter

_____

_____

Clothing/Coverings ☐
Waterproof ☐
Animal proof ☐
Sunproof ☐
Fire Started ☐

Food Inventory

Rations ☐

_____
_____
_____
_____

Water ☐
Hunting ☐

_____
_____
_____

Fishing ☐

_____
_____
_____

Foraging ☐

_____
_____
_____

Journey

Distance Covered

Trail Markers Used

Landmarks Sighted

Animal Prints

Map Sketch

Lat. _____ Long. _____

Party Member	Status	Injuries	Treatment

Date _____

Conditions

Weather

Terrain

Shelter

Shelter Constructed ☐

Type of Shelter

_____

_____

_____

Clothing/Coverings ☐

Waterproof ☐

Animal proof ☐

Sunproof ☐

Fire Started ☐

Food Inventory

Rations ☐

_____
_____
_____
_____

Water ☐

Hunting ☐

_____
_____
_____

Fishing ☐

_____
_____
_____

Foraging ☐

_____
_____
_____

Journey

Distance Covered

Trail Markers Used

Landmarks Sighted

Animal Prints

Map Sketch

Lat. _____ Long. _____

Party Member	Status	Injuries	Treatment

Date _____

Conditions

Weather

Terrain

Shelter

Shelter Constructed ☐

Type of Shelter

_____
_____

Clothing/Coverings ☐
Waterproof ☐
Animal proof ☐
Sunproof ☐
Fire Started ☐

Map Sketch

Lat. _____ Long. _____

Food Inventory

Rations ☐
_____
_____
_____
_____

Water ☐
Hunting ☐
_____
_____
_____

Fishing ☐
_____
_____

Foraging ☐
_____
_____

Journey

Distance Covered

Trail Markers Used

Landmarks Sighted

Animal Prints

Party Member	Status	Injuries	Treatment

Date _____

Conditions

Weather

Terrain

Shelter

Shelter Constructed ☐

Type of Shelter

_____

_____

Clothing/Coverings ☐
Waterproof ☐
Animal proof ☐
Sunproof ☐
Fire Started ☐

Food Inventory

Rations ☐

_____
_____
_____
_____

Water ☐
Hunting ☐

_____
_____
_____

Fishing ☐

_____
_____
_____

Foraging ☐

_____
_____
_____

Journey

Distance Covered

Trail Markers Used

Landmarks Sighted

Animal Prints

Map Sketch

Lat. _____ Long. _____

Party Member	Status	Injuries	Treatment

Date _____

Conditions

Weather

Terrain

Shelter

Shelter Constructed ☐

Type of Shelter

_____

_____

_____

Clothing/Coverings ☐

Waterproof ☐

Animal proof ☐

Sunproof ☐

Fire Started ☐

Food Inventory

Rations ☐

_____
_____
_____
_____

Water ☐

Hunting ☐

_____
_____
_____

Fishing ☐

_____
_____
_____

Foraging ☐

_____
_____
_____

Journey

Distance Covered

Trail Markers Used

Landmarks Sighted

Animal Prints

Map Sketch

Lat. _____   Long. _____

Party Member	Status	Injuries	Treatment

Date _____

Conditions

Weather

Terrain

Shelter

Shelter Constructed ☐

Type of Shelter

_____
_____
_____

Clothing/Coverings ☐
Waterproof ☐
Animal proof ☐
Sunproof ☐
Fire Started ☐

Food Inventory

Rations ☐
_____
_____
_____
_____

Water ☐
Hunting ☐
_____
_____
_____

Fishing ☐
_____
_____

Foraging ☐
_____
_____
_____

Map Sketch

Lat. _____   Long. _____

Journey

Distance Covered

Trail Markers Used

Landmarks Sighted

Animal Prints

Party Member	Status	Injuries	Treatment

Date _____

Conditions

Weather

Terrain

Shelter

Shelter Constructed ☐

Type of Shelter

_____

_____

Clothing/Coverings ☐
Waterproof ☐
Animal proof ☐
Sunproof ☐
Fire Started ☐

Map Sketch

Lat. _____ Long. _____

Food Inventory

Rations ☐
_____
_____
_____
_____

Water ☐
Hunting ☐
_____
_____
_____

Fishing ☐
_____
_____

Foraging ☐
_____
_____
_____

Journey

Distance Covered

Trail Markers Used

Landmarks Sighted

Animal Prints

Party Member	Status	Injuries	Treatment

Date _____

Conditions

Weather

Terrain

Shelter

Shelter Constructed ☐

Type of Shelter

_____

_____

Clothing/Coverings ☐

Waterproof ☐

Animal proof ☐

Sunproof ☐

Fire Started ☐

Food Inventory

Rations ☐

_____
_____
_____
_____

Water ☐
Hunting ☐

_____
_____
_____

Fishing ☐

_____
_____

Foraging ☐

_____
_____
_____

Journey

Distance Covered

Trail Markers Used

Landmarks Sighted

Animal Prints

Map Sketch

Lat. _____ Long. _____

Party Member	Status	Injuries	Treatment

Date _____

Conditions

Weather

Terrain

Shelter

Shelter Constructed ☐

Type of Shelter

_____

_____

_____

Clothing/Coverings ☐

Waterproof ☐

Animal proof ☐

Sunproof ☐

Fire Started ☐

Food Inventory

Rations ☐

_____
_____
_____
_____

Water ☐

Hunting ☐

_____
_____
_____

Fishing ☐

_____
_____
_____

Foraging ☐

_____
_____
_____

Map Sketch

Lat. _____ Long. _____

Journey

Distance Covered

Trail Markers Used

Landmarks Sighted

Animal Prints

Party Member	Status	Injuries	Treatment

Date _____

Conditions

Weather

Terrain

Food Inventory

Rations ☐

_____
_____
_____
_____

Water ☐
Hunting ☐

_____
_____
_____

Fishing ☐

_____
_____

Foraging ☐

_____
_____
_____

Journey

Distance Covered

Trail Markers Used

Landmarks Sighted

Animal Prints

Shelter

Shelter Constructed ☐

Type of Shelter
_____
_____
_____

Clothing/Coverings ☐
Waterproof ☐
Animal proof ☐
Sunproof ☐
Fire Started ☐

Map Sketch

Lat. _____ Long. _____

Party Member	Status	Injuries	Treatment

Date _____

Conditions

Weather

Terrain

Food Inventory

Rations ☐
_____
_____
_____
_____

Water ☐
Hunting ☐
_____
_____
_____

Fishing ☐
_____
_____
_____

Foraging ☐
_____
_____
_____

Journey

Distance Covered

Trail Markers Used

Landmarks Sighted

Animal Prints

Shelter

Shelter Constructed ☐

Type of Shelter
_____
_____

Clothing/Coverings ☐
Waterproof ☐
Animal proof ☐
Sunproof ☐
Fire Started ☐

Map Sketch

Lat. _____   Long. _____

Party Member	Status	Injuries	Treatment

www.ingramcontent.com/pod-product-compliance
Lightning Source LLC
LaVergne TN
LVHW060140080526
838202LV00049B/4039